Dawid Skrobiszewski

THE NAZI IDEOLOGY AND MEDICAL EXPERIMENTS AS A SYMBOL OF THE HUMAN TRAGEDY

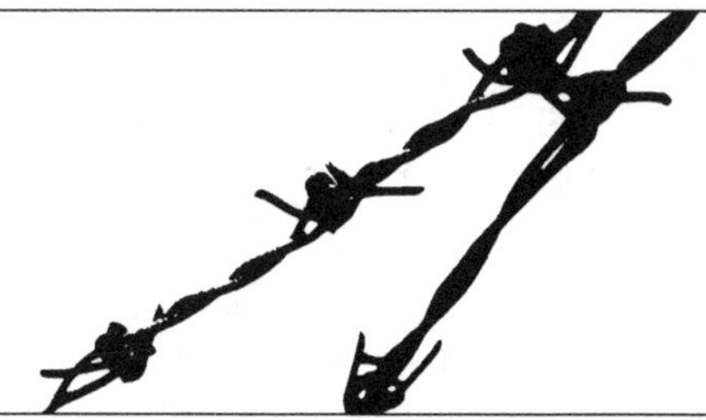

A PAST WE MUST NOT FORGET

ISBN 978-83-970326-1-3

Jeżewo (Poland 2024)

Contents

Reasons for writing the publication

My name is Dawid Skrobiszewski and I am a secondary school history teacher in a small town in northern Poland. My personal motivation for writing the following publication was a school trip. Together with my students, I went to the Auschwitz-Birkenau National Museum of Remembrance, a former Nazi concentration camp operated during the Second World War. Our group consisted of 45 people aged between 15 and 18. There I had the opportunity to see many young people of different nationalities listening intently to the camp guides with headphones. During the four-hour tour of the camp, I heard people speaking English, German, Polish, Spanish, Italian, Hebrew and languages spoken in Asian countries. I listened to their conversations and watched the expressions on their faces. I quickly realised that most of them had no idea of what had happened in the past and why Nazi camps had been created. As soon as I visited the camp and talked to my students, it was clear that the trip had aroused strong emotions in them, but they did not have much knowledge about the origins of the place. On their return, they asked many questions: 'Why?', 'What happened then?', 'How did it happen?'. They said: 'But it happened recently...', 'I have such a gentle nature, I'm good to people, so I won't let any extreme ideology manipulate me'. Is that so? The fact is that these atrocities happened very recently. People who lived through the Second World War are still alive today.

Today's globalised generation, with unlimited access to the world, does not reflect on historical tragedy on a daily basis.

If you put together contemporary ideas and new trends, you will suddenly find people today who say: 'That's the past, let's leave it behind...', 'Why reflect and dwell on what happened in the past?', 'The most important thing is the present and the future'. Dear reader, have you ever heard the sayings 'Those who don't remember history are condemned to relive it'[1] or 'History repeats itself'[2]? What do you think of them? Are they just empty words? I have to upset you... they are not just empty words and idle talk. History has repeated itself many times throughout history and there is much to learn from it.

The teaching of history is losing ground in schools around the world. Political squabbles between left-wing and right-wing political parties and changes in the education system are not helping. In some European countries it is not always possible to cover the 20th century in the classroom, and those who do not take an interest in the 20th century themselves may live in ignorance of why it is that they live in such a world. Indeed... I know this from my own experience! In a Polish school, an overloaded curriculum and learning unnecessary things is a common problem. My friends who work as teachers in different European countries confirm these facts. They know both the Polish and foreign education systems. Sarcastically speaking, prehistory and the Stone Age, the Neolithic Revolution from distant historical periods should be more important for modern people. A more important topic to study should be ancient Phoenicia and the creation of its alphabet, or the domestication of the cat in ancient times. Surely a more important issue for humanity is the medieval manor than the tragedy of one's grandparents and great-grandparents living in the 20th century. Is what I am writing about not absurd? I will leave a big question mark here so that you can answer that question for yourself. It is not my intention to complain about the European education system. My job is to answer the questions that young people have asked me.

Dear reader, I am not a great, outstanding expert or scholar. I don't have a respectable academic title (unless you count a Master's degree). I am just like you, a person who goes to work

---

[1] The words of American philosopher George Santayana.

[2] The quotation is not attributed to a famous thinker. The phrase is known around the world. It is popular with many politicians, philosophers or historians. It is probably a modified form of another maxim, 'Fortune is like a wheel', which was used in ancient times and is attested by Cicero, among others.

every day and likes to go out with friends from time to time. In my spare time, I watch a series or a film on television or read a book. In this publication, I would like to share with you what I know and what I think is important for you to understand what happened during the turbulent period of the 20th century. Think of me as a friend who has something important to tell you, who doesn't want to bore you with the history of the nations. I want to use my knowledge and my modest writing skills to help you better understand the world as your place on earth. It won't be a study where I show off my historical knowledge. I just want to add to your knowledge and make you aware of how the world looked like in those years. I also want to give my students, but also students from other schools around the world, answers to the unanswered questions left in the Auschwitz-Birkenau Museum. I would like to reach as many people as possible and to satisfy their natural human curiosity.

My intention is not to insult or ridicule any nation. I am not a Polish nationalist and I have no xenophobic views. Having been brought up with European values, I respect the modern European heritage and believe that all nations should respect each other, no matter what they have been through together.

Contemporary online sources contain a great deal of material on topics related to the 20th century war time, but with so many websites and articles available, I wanted to select the most relevant and summarise them. I tried to find a compromise between a multi-page history book (which is what you usually get) and a short historical study. I hope you will like it, especially as this is the first book I have ever written.

Today, the subject of the Second World War is alluded to in the mass media and in politics. There are still unhealed wounds from the past between states. Our task is to find out how these wounds came about and to heal them as soon as possible. Without basic knowledge, we have no chance of doing so.

It is also worth mentioning issues of unawareness, ignorance or misrepresentation of historical truth. In the 21st century, the terms 'Polish concentration camps' and 'Polish death camps' appear quite often in the media around the world. For example, in 2018, a detailed study prepared by the Polish portal 'Polityka w Sieci' showed that on 27 January that year, there were between 23 and 28 million views of the term 'Polish death camps' on the internet worldwide. At its peak, there were 9.1 tweets per minute on Twitter. By comparison, the term 'German death camps' reached around one million impressions on the same day[3]. US President Barack Obama used the phrase 'Polish death camp' at a White House ceremony on 29 May 2012.

The fact that in the 21st century alone so many journalists, academics and politicians have uttered the words 'Polish extermination camps' can only be evidence of under information or deliberate actions that negatively affect historical truth. It is our duty to reject untruths and to rely on facts. An indisputable argument is the fact that when German (Nazi) concentration camps or extermination/ death camps were created, the Polish state simply did not exist (it was deprived of its statehood)! Is this so strange? Of course not! There were times in the history of the Polish nation when it did not have a state. This was the case from 1795 to 1918 and from October 1939 to 1944, and Poland was oppressed by the communist regime until 1989. It could be said that from the 1st September 1939 (the date of the outbreak of the Second World War, i.e. the date of the German aggression against Poland) its territory shrank every day in favour of Nazi Germany[4]. It was from this time that the camps began to be built on Polish land. This begs the question: how could they have been Polish when there was no Polish state? Dear reader, this is an undeniable fact and do not be misled by the phrase 'Polish extermination camps' or 'Polishconcentration camps' etc.

In my work, I describe the greatest turmoil and crimes of totalitarian fascist ideology that befell the human race in the 20th century. The culmination was in the years 1933-1945, when the

---

[3] Ibidem.

[4] From 17 September 1939, also in favour of the USSR from the east.

German concentration, extermination and work camps existed. I also wanted to present a chronological sequence of the most important facts of the inter-war period. This publication deals with questions from various fields of scholarship. Historical questions are at the forefront, interwoven with medical and biological questions. It presents the chronological development of the Third Reich's policy on the purity of the Aryan race and the elimination of nations hated by Hitler. Jews, Gypsies and Slavic tribes were used in the brutal policy of racial purity. It was a long-term process that was to bring success to German society.

In the introduction and the first chapter of the book, I want to answer the reader's questions about what led to the outbreak of the greatest war of the 20th century, the Second World War. The first chapter also deals with the set of ideas, beliefs, concepts and methods of Nazi politics. It also gives a brief history of the emergence of fascism in Europe. Issues such as the Nazis' attitudes towards other races, religions and homosexuals are covered in this chapter. I also describe Germany's population policy and the guiding idea of the slavery of other nations, and deal with the problems of eugenics in Germany from the beginning to the end of 1945. In the second chapter I describe in detail the medical experiments carried out on prisoners in the German camps. The book's chapters are divided according to the selected camps and the experiments performed on humans.

What questions will you find answers to after reading this book? Here are some of them:

- What was the world like and how did it evolve after the First World War?
- What were the origins of fascism in the Old Continent?
- What were the characteristics of a totalitarian state?
- What was it that drove the Nazis to these horrific acts?
- What was German imperialist policy and the assumptions of the so-called 'Lebensraum' ('living space')?
- What were the Nazis' views on population policy in their country?

- What was the eugenics policy of the German state from its foundation until 1945?
- Who did the Nazis want to get rid of in their ideal world and why?
- What was the system of concentration and extermination camps like?
- What experiments were carried out on prisoners in German camps?
- What were the consequences of the medical experiments?
- In which camps were medical experiments carried out?
- How did Europe and the world change after the Second World War?

I wanted to present all this in an interesting and understandable language for the reader. I minimised scientific terms and tried to explain difficult cases in a clear and transparent way. In some chapters I had to use data from other scientific or internet sources. I hope that after reading this book you will find answers to your questions. I will probably surprise you more than once with many interesting facts from the turbulent interwar period and the Second World War.

Please join me in reflecting on this history. Here we go.

Introduction

The world after the First World War
Before Hitler's ideology

Before moving on to the main topic, I would like to describe the geopolitical and social reality of Europe and the world after 1918. The First World War, which lasted from 1914 to 1918 and is known throughout the world as the 'Great War, left its mark on world history (the main fighting took place on the European continent). As soon as this global conflict came to an end, the Old Continent[5] was plunged into political, social and economic chaos. It is estimated that around 15 million people died in the conflict, including 5 million civilians[6]. It should be noted that proportionally more soldiers died than civilians (2x1 ratio). However, the number of wounded was even higher. There were millions of crippled men in Europe - wounded on the war front. European armies stagnated as many military commanders died as a result of the conflict. Europe was devastated not only by bombing, but also by other forms of warfare. Many areas of Europe needed extensive reconstruction. Immediately afterwards, Europe was hit by the deadly Spanish flu pandemic, which killed between 50 and 80 million people[7]. The disease spread from 1918 to the mid-1920s. Disease itself claimed a far greater number of victims than the war itself. One can only imagine what the world looked like with the pandemic and the war.

As soon as the wars ended, peace treaties were signed. On 28 June 1919, after the First World War, a key document known in world history as the Treaty of Versailles was signed. This peace treaty declared that the country of Germany was solely to blame for the Great War, which meant that

---

[5]   The Old Continent - synonymous with Europe.

[6]   D. Skrobiszewski, *Pandemie XX i XXI wieku*, Bydgoszcz 2012, p. 21.

[7]   Ibidem.

the country had to take responsibility for all the loss and destruction. The peace treaty imposed severe penalties and sanctions on Germany, including[8].

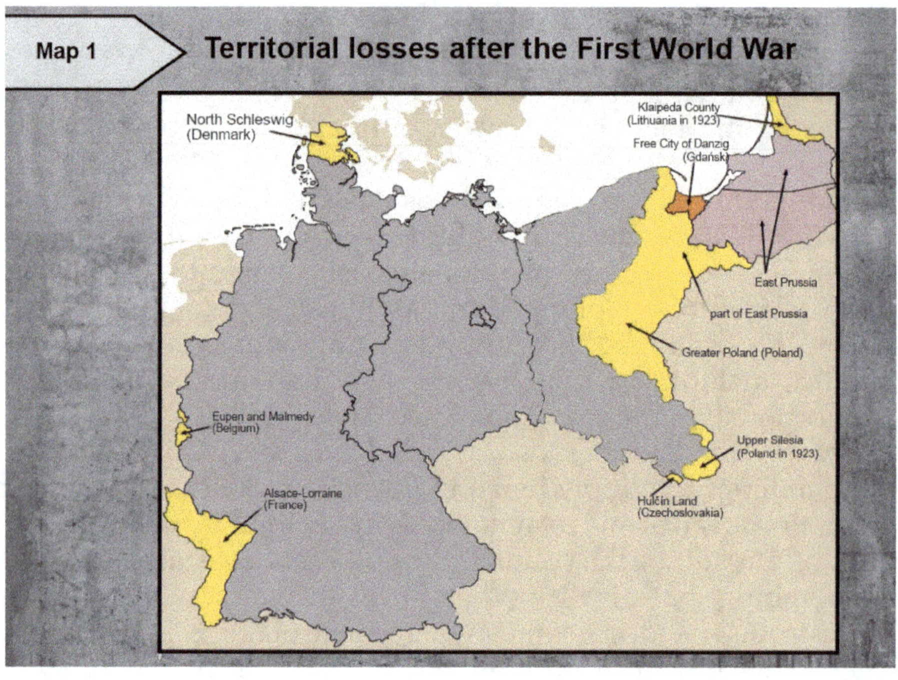

[9]

Under the terms of the Treaty of Versailles, Germany was obliged to return Alsace and Lorraine to France. Belgium received two border districts from Germany, Eupen and Malmedy, and Denmark received the northern part of Schleswig after a plebiscite in 1920. Czechoslovakia received part of Upper Silesia (Hulčín Land). Poland gained access to the Baltic Sea, creating the area known as East Prussia. The Saarland was to be placed under League of Nations administration for 15 years, after which a national vote was

---

[8]   This day was declared a National Day of Mourning by the German Protestant Church.

[9]   Map created under the CC BY-SA 3.0 Wikimedia Commons licence, public domain.

to be held to decide whether these areas should remain with Germany or fall to France. Germany also lost its overseas colonies to France and Britain.

The provisions of this document imposed a number of military restrictions on Germany. The size of the German army was limited to 100,000 men, and the introduction of universal conscription was prohibited. The country's armed forces were deprived of the right to possess submarines, tanks and aircraft, while the number of warships was limited to 36 small units. A demilitarised zone was established on the left bank of the Rhine and a 50-kilometre strip on the right bank. These measures were designed to limit Germany's military power in order to avoid future retaliation. Economic burdens were also imposed on Germany in the form of war reparations[10] to compensate for the losses suffered by other countries. The value of reparations was set at 132 billion marks ($33 billion), to be paid in gold. This huge sum was intended to limit the growth of Germany's economic power and ensure that the country would not be able to recover economically from its defeat in the First World War. The issue of war reparations is dealt with in Part VIII of the Treaty. The obligation to pay reparations is set out in Art. 232: '(...) The Allied and

---

[10] Reparation - war compensation.

Associated Governments claim, and Germany undertakes, to make reparations for all damage caused to their civilian populations and to their property during the period in which each of the Allied and Associated Powers was at war with Germany by the aforesaid attack by land, sea and air, and in general for all damage specified in Annex I (...)'[11]. It was agreed that France would receive 52%, England 22%, Italy 10% and Belgium 8% of the total war reparations. Portugal and Japan were to receive 0.75% each, while the remaining 6.5% was to be divided between Greece, Romania, Yugoslavia and other eligible countries under separate agreements[12].

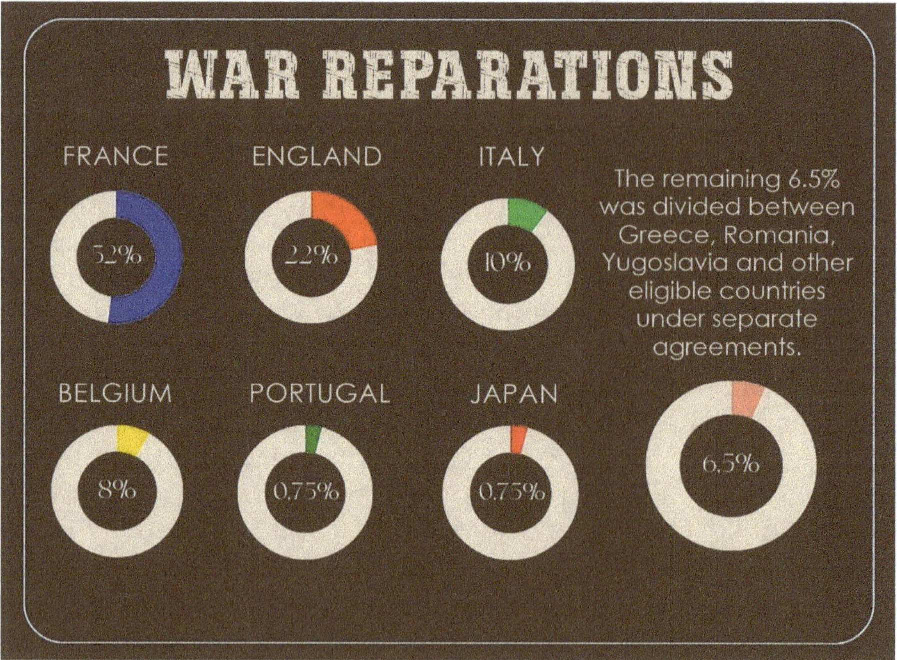

Chart 1. War reparations according to the Treaty of Versailles.

---

[11] Art. 232 *Treaty of Peace between the Allied and Associated Powers and Germany*. Versailles. 28 June 1919.

[12] T. Kotłowski, *Problem niemieckich reparacji po I wojnie światowej*, Poznań 2014, p. 3.

During the 1920s, the rules for compensation payments were changed twice, slightly reducing the total amount to 112 billion marks paid in gold. By 1932, the German state had paid about 25-30% of the amount originally agreed[13]. After Hitler came to power, payments were stopped. Officially, Germany repaid the full amount of war reparations from the First World War in 2010, 92 years after the end of the bloody conflict[14]. The new countries created after the war (see below) did not receive any money for war damage.

The German delegation tried unsuccessfully to water down the agreement, but all that resulted was a threat that the Allies might occupy German territory. Throughout the country these suggestions caused shock and anger, with the draft terms seen as a manifestation of injustice. The Treaty of Versailles was seen in Germany as an expression of vindictiveness on the part of the victorious Allies, with long-term financial commitments discouraging the country from economic initiative. Almost 13% of the German population suddenly found themselves outside the former Reich. The presence of German populations in Alsace, Lorraine, parts of the Rhineland and areas of Silesia, Pomerania, Poland and Czechoslovakia led to conflict and encouraged the growth of German nationalist sentiment.

In conclusion, **the Treaty of Versailles**, although intended to bring peace and stability, **contributed to tensions**. German discontent and an atmosphere of hatred led to the outbreak of **the Second World War**. The new agreement was supposed to end the war, but it had a destabilising effect on Europe and created the conditions for **national conflicts**.

---

[13] Ibidem.

[14] The German state paid off the war debts covered by the agreement by the early 1980s. After the reunification of the country in 1990, Germany continued to issue 20-year bonds to pay off the remaining interest on the war reparations. Their repayment ended in 2010, on 3 October.

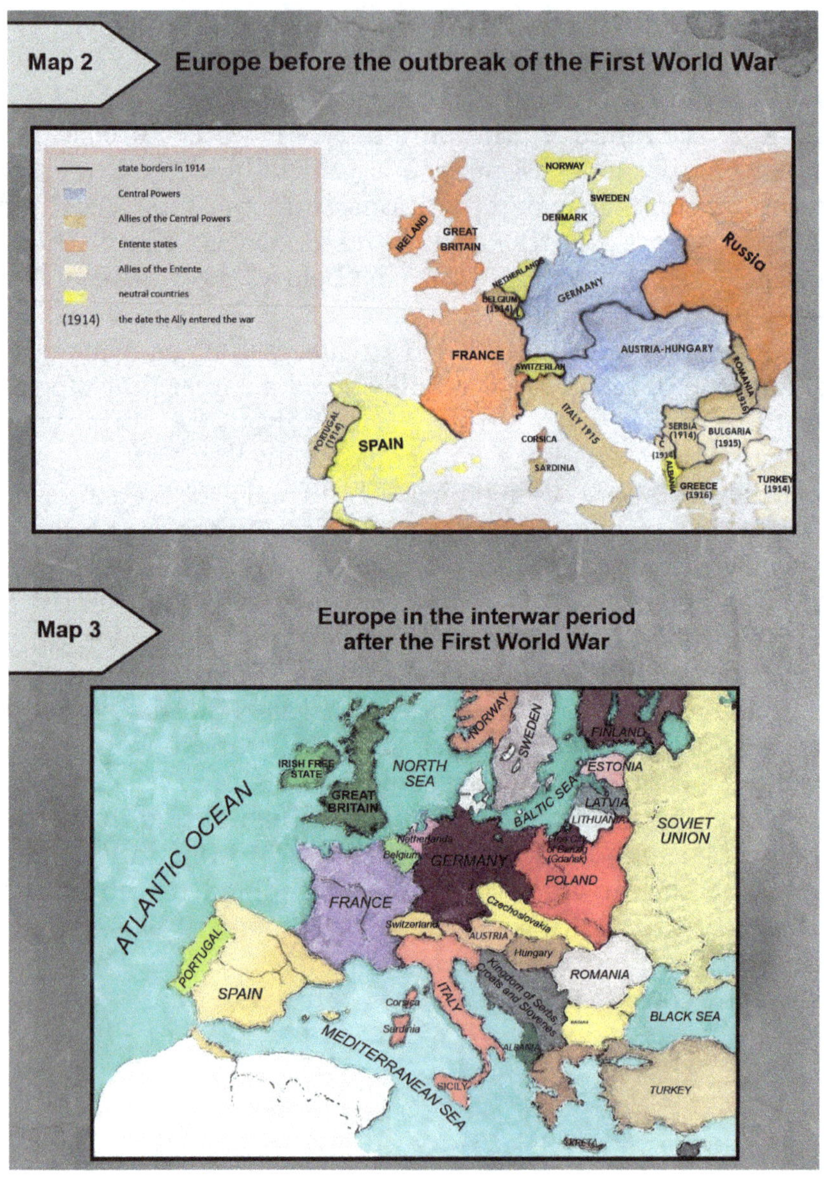

Map 2
Europe before the outbreak of the First World War

state borders in 1914
Central Powers
Allies of the Central Powers
Entente states
Allies of the Entente
neutral countries
(1914)   the date the Ally entered the war

NORWAY
SWEDEN
DENMARK
IRELAND
GREAT BRITAIN
NETHERLANDS
BELGIUM (1914)
GERMANY
Russia
FRANCE
SWITZERLAND
AUSTRIA-HUNGARY
ROMANIA (1916)
ITALY 1915
PORTUGAL (1916)
SPAIN
CORSICA
SARDINIA
SERBIA (1914)
ALBANIA (1914)
BULGARIA (1915)
GREECE (1916)
TURKEY (1914)

Map 3
Europe in the interwar period
after the First World War

ATLANTIC OCEAN
IRISH FREE STATE
GREAT BRITAIN
NORTH SEA
NORWAY
SWEDEN
BALTIC SEA
FINLAND
ESTONIA
LATVIA
LITHUANIA
SOVIET UNION
Netherlands
Belgium
GERMANY
Free City of Danzig (Gdańsk)
POLAND
FRANCE
Switzerland
Czechoslovakia
AUSTRIA
Hungary
ROMANIA
Kingdom of Serbs, Croats and Slovenes
PORTUGAL
SPAIN
Corsica
Sardinia
ITALY
ALBANIA
SICILY
MEDITERRANEAN SEA
BLACK SEA
TURKEY
CRETE

15

Another consequence of the First World War and the peace treaty was the creation of new states in Europe. Many powers lost territory. The countries created after 1918 were Poland, Czechoslovakia, Austria and Hungary (the collapse of Austria-Hungary), Lithuania, Latvia, Estonia, Finland, SHS - the Kingdom of Serbs, Croats and Slovenes[16]. This list also includes the Union of Soviet Socialist Republics (USSR), which existed from 1922 right after the suppression of the revolution and civil war in Russia.

As we can see from Map 3, all the new countries created after the First World War are mainly located in the central and eastern part of the European continent. I must point out that the countries created after the First World War already existed in the past. They had their own history, but for various reasons, including partition or annexation, they became part of larger powers. But the moment just after the war was not the moment of their original creation. The best example from 'my backyard' is Poland, which was partitioned three times in the 18th century, with Prussia, Austria and Russia as partitioners and later invaders.

The victorious powers, known as the Entente, which mainly included France, Britain and Russia, and outside Europe the United States, decided on changes to national borders. These European states influenced the terms of the Treaty of Versailles. Nevertheless, after the First World War, other independent states emerged in the world, such as Georgia, Armenia, Moldova, Iceland and Mongolia. In 1921, Ireland gained partial independence from Great Britain, creating the Irish Free State and later Northern Ireland. Many of the new states were made up of different ethnic groups. Building unitary states was very difficult, especially when there were tensions between different ethnic groups.

If you don't know what it's about, it's about money

After the end of the First World War and the establishment of the new world order, many countries faced an economic

---

[16] From 1929 - the country was called Yugoslavia.

crisis. Destruction, huge war debts, inflation and loss of markets left the economies of many countries in a critical state. A prime example is the Weimar Republic of Germany, which experienced economic hardship and hyperinflation[17] very soon after the signing of the Treaty of Versailles.

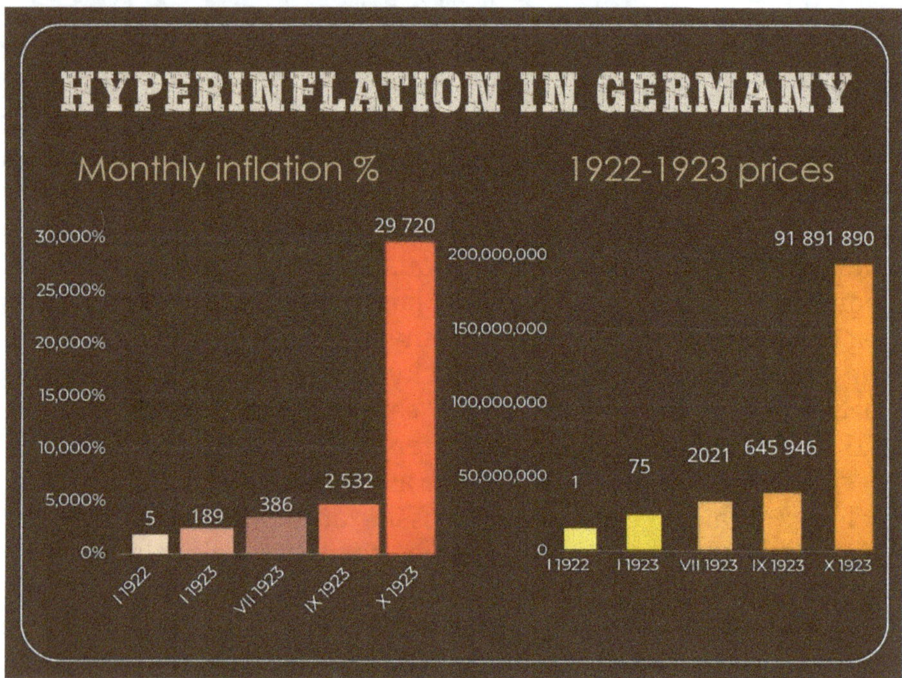

Chart 2. Hyperinflation in Germany (1922-1923)[18]

From the above graph, it can be concluded that the war reparations settlement contributed to the financial crisis in Germany.

During the interwar period (1918-1939) the world was changing. Societies were slowly rebuilding their economic and social potential. There was a rapid growth of technology and science in the world, when suddenly something very

---

[17] Hyperinflation - extreme inflation.

[18] Own elaboration, source: Encyklopedia PWN, entry: Hiperinflacja w Niemczech (accessed 20/11/2023).

disturbing happened. The great economic crisis, known as the Great Depression, broke out in the United States, starting on 24 October 1929 in New York City. This date is known in history as 'Black Thursday'. It was the worst economic crisis in history and had a profound effect on the economies of countries around the world. The crisis ended in 1933. It began with the collapse of the stock market on Wall Street in New York. Within days, panic gripped the entire market, leading to sharp falls in share prices and huge financial losses for investors. The Great Depression was the result of deep-seated structural problems in the US economy, such as excessive stock market speculation, huge debts, trade imbalances, overproduction in certain sectors and social inequalities. In addition, the crisis was worsened by the bankruptcy of many banks and companies that were unable to pay their debts. During the Great Depression, there was a sharp decline in the dynamism of industrial production.

The effects of the Great Depression included bankruptcies and increased debt for companies and societies as a whole. Millions of people around the world lost their jobs, leading to social imbalances - first in the US and later globally as the crisis spread very quickly to other continents. Unemployment soared and millions of people lost their jobs. Unemployment in the US reached around 25% during the worst of the crisis. The unemployed were unable to support themselves and their families, leading to a significant increase in poverty and the need for government assistance. People approached life with pessimism and frustration.

Photo 1. The photograph shows two men looking for work during the Great Depression in the USA[19].

Europe after the Great Depression

The consequences of the crisis have also had an impact on the political situation. The recession led to the collapse of many parliamentary democracies in favour of authoritarian or dictatorial systems. Germany was one of the countries hardest hit by unemployment, with almost half of the working age population (around 43%!) unemployed in 1932[20]. Despite high unemployment, many countries did not pursue an active fiscal policy on benefits. Even when such a programme was introduced in one country, it was short-term and severely limited the provision of basic needs for many families. During this period, the crisis not only affected national economies

---

[19] Photo: public domain.

[20] https://facinghistory.org/resource-library (accessed 23/11/2023).

but was also a major factor in the emergence of radical social and political movements. The Nazi Party in Germany gained a dominant position by exploiting public dissatisfaction with poverty, unemployment and lack of prospects. A society tired of difficult living conditions and poor prospects for the future leaned towards populist slogans of rebuilding economic power. German society also identified with the fight against perceived enemies, which for Adolf Hitler and his party were the Jewish community and the Communists. This in turn led to a new conflict. Germany's imperialist ambitions became entangled with deep-rooted prejudices and a sense of injustice (see Chapter I). Another country where the Great Depression affected the political situation was Spain. The economic recession contributed to the collapse of the monarchy and the establishment of the Second Spanish Republic in 1931. As a result, civil war broke out in Spain in 1936, after which General Francisco Franco took over as dictator.

In October 1933, the atmosphere escalated when Germany, already under Hitler, withdrew from the League of Nations, which it had joined in 1926. In March 1935, Germany gradually began to violate the principles of the Treaty of Versailles by creating its own armed forces. Although there was a risk of armed conflict, Hitler judged the situation perfectly, recognising that Britain and France, as guarantors of peace, would not risk a decision leading to a new conflict, given the trauma of the Great Depression and the experience of the First World War. The consequence of such a policy was the subjugation of the Rhineland demilitarised zone by the German state, which once again put Europe on the brink of potential war. The balance in Europe was once again disrupted. France decided to ask the League of Nations to condemn Germany's actions. However, the resolutions of the League, which had no military response of its own, made no impression on Hitler. Ignoring other countries, the Third Reich went on to develop its wartime potential. At the end of August 1936, Hitler ordered full war preparedness to be achieved by the end of 1940. From the autumn of 1936, Germany supported Francisco Franco's military actions in the Spanish Civil War. On 25 November that year, an agreement was reached between the countries that had withdrawn from the League of Nations. Germany and Japan signed the Anti-Comintern Pact, pledging to fight communism together. A year later, fascist Italy joined it, and in March 1939 - Spain, under the government of F. Franco. After these events, Hitler, seeing the reaction of the European states, which did not really oppose his policy, continued to pursue his aims and desires, this time appealing to the principle of the self-determination of nations. In March 1938, he carried out the 'Anschluss', in other words, he simply incorporated Austria into his country. Europe still did not intervene, believing that Hitler was merely trying to unite the entire German nation.

The last act of the German leader before the outbreak of the Second World War was to 'liberate' the German minority from the oppression of the Czechoslovak government and its territorial claims. In the 'name of peace', Britain and France decided to persuade Czechoslovakia to make concessions to Hitler. On 21 September 1938, Czechoslovakia agreed to cede its border territories to Germany. This seems surprising years later, as Czechoslovakia had a relatively strong and modern army. The country had a significant number of well-trained soldiers and modern weaponry, including tanks and artillery. The system of fortifications known as the 'Benes Line' was one of the most advanced in Europe. These fortifications, mainly along the border with Germany, were designed to delay or stop a potential attack from that country. It is now arguable that Czechoslovakia could, in theory, have successfully repelled a potential German attack. So why did it not do so? Although Czechoslovakia was militarily prepared to defend itself, the lack of international support and pressure from Hitler and his allies, especially the Italians, left Czechoslovakia paralysed and suffocating under the pressure of the fascist countries. In order to keep the peace, a conference was organised in Munich under the leadership of his Italian ally Benito Mussolini. On 29 September of the same year, British Prime Minister Neville Chamberlain, French Prime Minister Edward Daladier, Adolf Hitler and Benito Mussolini signed a treaty providing for the immediate surrender of Czechoslovakia to Germany[21].

In fact, Poland and Hungary also benefited by annexing parts of Czechoslovakia. It seemed that the situation in Europe had stabilised and that Germany would give up its claims to other territories. They were wrong, as Hitler persuaded Slovakia to break away from Bohemia and form a separate state. This happened on 14 March 1939. Intimidated by the bombing of Prague, Czechoslovak President Emil Hácha and Foreign Minister František Chvalkovský signed a document in Berlin on 15 March placing the 'fate of the Czech nation and country' in Hitler's hands. There, the Germans established the Protectorate of Bohemia and Moravia, which became completely dependent on them[22]. Eight days later, the Germans forced Lithuania to surrender Klaipėda and the Klaipėda region (which had been abandoned by Germany after the First World War and annexed by the Lithuanians in January 1923).

---

[21] https://historia.org.pl/2009/09/07/hanba-monachijska-1938 (accessed 22/11/2023).
[22] https://praguemorning.cz/march-15-1939-when-hitler-marched-into-czechoslovakia-RPu7WZG9iE (accessed 22/11/2023).

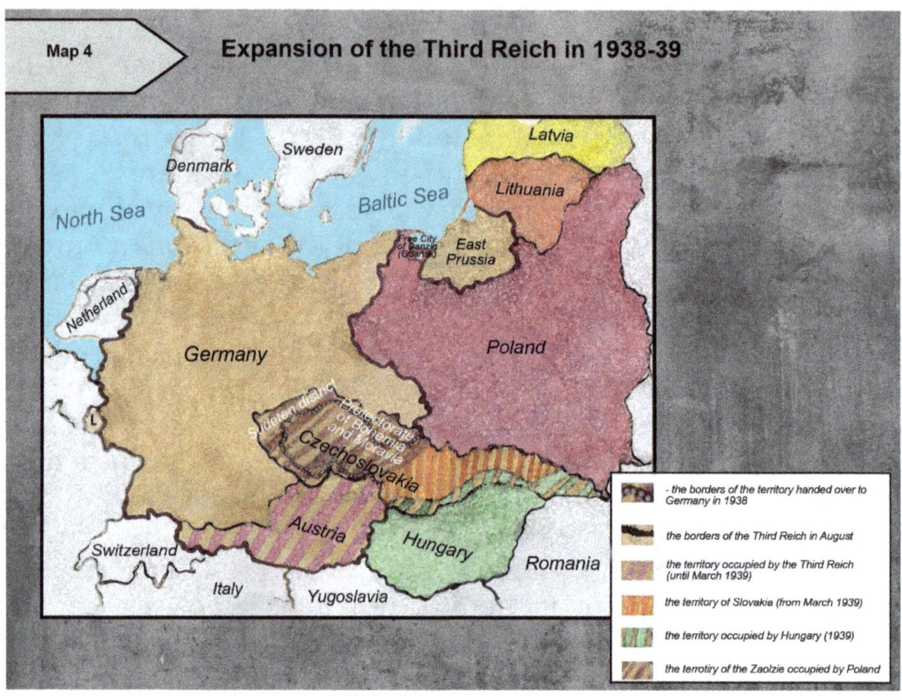

23

Even before the outbreak of war, there were claims against Poland. In January and March 1939, Poland refused to extend the non-aggression pact of 26 January 1934 for 25 years, as well as the joint 'anti-Russian combination' offered by the Third Reich. In exchange for a 25-year extension of the non-aggression pact, a joint 'anti-Russian combination', and a free port and railway for Poles in Gdańsk, Germany demanded that Poland be allowed to incorporate Gdańsk into the Third Reich and to build an extraterritorial motorway and railway line through Gdańsk Pomerania to East Prussia (the Polish border in this area of the Baltic Sea divided the territory of the Reich). Poland strongly opposed such proposals, believing that acceptance of these provisions would be tantamount to a loss of the country's independence and sovereignty. This Polish

---

[23] Own map.

position was the first clear rejection of Germany's expansionist policy. Hitler quickly came to an agreement with the Soviet Union, signing a non-aggression pact and the division of Polish lands on 23 August 1939, after defeating that country in the war. This agreement is known in history as the Molotov-Ribbentrop Pact. This agreement was designed to divide the roles of the states in Eastern Europe and thus contributed to the outbreak of the Second World War, which began on 1 September 1939 with German aggression against Poland.

'So the war...'.

Dear reader, I hope I have given you a brief overview of the geopolitical situation in the interwar period. I have focused on areas of Europe, because on this continent an ideology emerged which soon had a significant impact on the lives of millions of lives and future generations. I want to prove that different ideologies change the course of history. The First World War, the entire interwar period, the Second World War and the immediate post-war aftermath all made their own contribution to the shape of the world today. It is worth understanding that the contemporary geopolitical situation is the result of many historical, social and political factors of that period. History continually provides us with lessons that can serve as a guide for action in the present and the future. Analysing past events and learning from them can lead us to a sustainable future.

Let's move on to Chapter I, where we examine the concepts, main assumptions and tools of Nazi ideology.

Chapter I

The concept of German fascism (Nazism)

How fascism emerged and became an ideology?

Let's start by clarifying what the word 'ideology' means. It is a term derived from the Greek 'idéa', meaning 'idea', and 'lógos', the word for 'science'[24]. An ideology is a set of values, beliefs, ideas and views that describe how we perceive reality. It is also a set of rules of behaviour for social movements and political parties. It consists of philosophical, economic, legal, ethical, religious and artistic concepts. The creators and followers of ideologies refer to the rights of the individual and his or her role in society, to the principles of state institutions, to changes in the existing social order, to freedom and justice. They say what changes need to be made to improve the world around us. They point to an idealistic goal to which society should aspire. Ideologies indicate the policies that must be implemented in order to achieve these goals. Ideologies are used as the basis for the programmes of political parties, which seek to achieve specific goals. Reference to ideology helps politicians to communicate with the public[25].

Fascism began in Italy in 1919, when Benito Mussolini founded the Union of Italian Combatants. After two years he transformed it into the National Fascist Party. At first, fascism was not associated with an ideology, but rather with political organisations and movements. It was associated with a method of gaining power. Sociopolitical views were shaped by the practices and actions of fascist leaders. It was Italian fascism that inspired organisations and political movements in other countries (e.g. Romania - Legion of the

---

[24]   https://ideologia.pl (accessed 24/11/2023).

[25]   Ibidem.

Archangel Michael, Spain - Falanga, Hungary - Arrow Crossers, United Kingdom - British Union of Fascists). However, the best-known fascist party was the National Socialist German Workers' Party - NSDAP. The fascist parties aimed to achieve and believed in different things. This depended on the specifics of the country in which they were based and operated. The basic assumptions were the principles of class solidarity, the cult of the leader and party centralisation.

Fascist ideologies are characterised by combining different views derived from other ideas. Fascism was mainly based on nationalism, national socialism, conservatism and racism. All of this was combined with the teachings of the philosophical systems of Friedrich Nietzsche and Georg Wilhelm F. Hegel. Fascism also drew on the history and traditions of its own peoples, but often idealised them. It emphasised a belief in the uniqueness of its people. The movement also promoted the idea of imperialism and domination over other nations. Fascism advocated strong leadership and a one-party state. Power in a state had to be concentrated in a single leader (chief) with a wide range of powers. Fascism was also characterised by a rejection of liberalism or individual freedom. It rejected all democratic principles and instead proposed a model of society based on centralisation under the strong leadership of a single party. All this was to be overseen by a militarily powerful army and police force as a means of maintaining internal order and guaranteeing the achievement of measured external goals. The economy and all private enterprise were also to be subordinated to the state. This ideology was perfectly described by **B. Mussolini**, who said: '**Everything within the State, nothing outside the State, nothing against the State**'[26]. 'Everything within the State' meant that the state was at the centre of social, economic and political life.

---

[26] The most famous sentence of B. Mussolini characterising totalitarianism was uttered on 28/10/1925 in Milan: 'Our method is this: everything within the State, nothing outside the State, nothing against the State'. source: Ł. Dominiak, Totalitaryzm, [in:] Encyklopedia Białych Plam, vol. 17, Radom 2006, p. 173.

All spheres of social life should be under the control of the state, which would direct them according to its own ideologies and goals. 'Nothing outside the State' referred to the rejection of the autonomy of communities or social institutions in favour of uniform control by the state. Other forms of social or economic organisation tended to be restricted or eliminated. 'Nothing against the State' - this part of the phrase suggests that any form of opposition or independence from the state is unacceptable. It implies that individuals and social groups should submit to the will of the state and that any form of resistance or criticism can be treated as dangerous and quickly eliminated. This approach of the Italian leader is characteristic of totalitarianism, where the state has control over all spheres of social, economic and political life. In practice, this meant a strong centralisation of power, repressive methods to maintain order, the elimination of opposition and a strong state involvement in the economy and individual lives.

Fascist doctrine is the cult of the strong state. Power was vested in the commander-in-chief and political decisions were made illegally. In the fascist state, the executive had greater powers. There were extensive spying and investigation apparatuses in the police authorities. The state took control of all social life and monitored people's behaviour, psyche and thoughts. A whole network of organisations was set up with the aim of activating society in a fascist direction. In interwar Italy, these principles were implemented by Benito Mussolini's government.

Photo 2. Benito Mussolini in 1940[27].

German fascism - Nazism (hitlerism) - national socialism

German fascism[28] was one of the most criminal regimes in human history. The origins of this system can be traced back to German history. The terms of the Treaty of Versailles humiliated the German people. For years they had aroused contempt and resentment towards other states and peoples. In addition, the economic crisis in Europe in the 1930s deepened resentment towards the political systems of the time. Germans did not agree with the postwar restrictions. There was also a crisis of religious values in the 1920s and 1930s. All this led people to act impulsively, driven by emotion.

---

[27] Photographer: H. Roger-Viollet. Source: https://commons.wikimedia.org/wiki/File:Benito_Mussolini_colored.jpg (accessed 16/11/2023).

[28] We can use synonyms for the term: Nazism, hitlerism, national socialism·

We can distinguish two reasons for the rise of German fascism:

The first reason was a psychological and historical concept derived from the German national tradition, according to which Nazism was 'the manifestation of aspirations and instincts flowing from the deepest strata of the Germanic soul'[29]. Nazism arose out of anti-democratic, anti-liberal and anti-individualist principles. Put simply, 'this is the nature of the German people'.

The second was the great economic crisis in Europe after the First World War. There was also the Spanish flu, which decimated populations across the continent. The result of these crises was a civilisational breakthrough in which new ideologies emerged. Their main aim was to overthrow democratic-liberal governments because it was believed that such a regime could not rebuild the world economy. This led to hitlerism in Germany and to internal transformations as a way of overcoming the moral, spiritual, economic and social crisis.

The extremes of Nazism were **pagan** and **anti-Catholic ideology**. Adolf Hitler believed that the Germanic race was superior to all nations. He considered the people of Eastern Europe, the Slavs, to be primarily a subspecies of man.

The Slavs inhabited the area to the east of Germany. They include: Poles, Czechs, Slovaks, Russians, Belarusians, Ukrainians, Serbs, Croats, Slovenes, Bulgarians, Bosnians, Macedonians and other smaller national groups.

From July 1933, when Adolf Hitler's party became the only legal party in Germany, hitlerism spread over a long period. As a national movement, Nazism counteracted the existing chaos and

---

[29] M. Musielak, *Nazizm w interpretacjach polskiej myśli politycznej okresu międzywojennego*, Poznań 1997, p. 18.

anarchy in the German state, which had arisen after the Great Depression. Other effects of this crisis were new social concepts that led to high unemployment and the collapse of democratic and parliamentary systems. The young generation believed that the nation should strive to unify feelings, thoughts and social ambitions. The assumptions of this ideology were not new. It was only the organisational units and methods that were innovative. Nazism and fascism had both similarities and differences[30]. The common thing was the creation of authority figures. The most important people in the party became leaders who demonstrated the ability to lead people.

Hitlerism developed and continued the ideas of traditional Germany. It was different from the needs and aspirations of other nations. This was because the German people were made up of different ethnic communities. Hitler wanted to unite his nation and prevent Germany from disintegrating internally, economically, politically and morally. In his view, national socialism promoted the fight against economic crisis and strengthened the organisation of the nation. Hitler targeted one nation in particular - the Jews.

Why?
One of the central elements of the Nazi concept was racism. The ideology of racism emerged in the mid-19th century. It received an unexpected boost after the First World War, exerting a strong influence on socio-political relations, particularly in Germany. Racist views became increasingly popular in Germany. Hitler wrote his thoughts on race in his book Mein Kampf, first published in 1925, arguing that human races differed in value, with the Aryan race being the highest and most valuable of all. The author developed his anti-Semitic beliefs extensively, blaming Jews for many social and economic problems. He regarded them as enemies of the German people and promoted conspiracy theories about their

---

[30] See Section 'The difference between Italian and German fascism'.

alleged control of the world. Importantly, Hitler promoted the idea of maintaining 'racial purity' through the use of eugenics laws[31] and by promoting and protecting the 'purity' of the German Aryan race.

The adoption of Nazism was also the myth of **the enemy of the nation.** The Führer decided who was to blame for Germany's problems, especially after the defeat in the First World War and the humiliating Treaty of Versailles. The Jews became a convenient target. Anti-Semitism became a tool for directing public anger and frustration at specific groups. The Jewish people in the interwar period did not have a state of their own and lived in territories all over the world. The largest group of Jews lived in Europe, where diasporas (Jewish communities) were formed. These beliefs were later reflected in the racial policies of the Third Reich, which led to the systematic genocide of the Jewish people. Hitler presented the concept of 'Lebensraum' (living space) as a justification for Germany's territorial expansion. He believed that expansion to the east was necessary to provide sufficient space for the expanding German Aryan race. Expansion was to be at the expense of other lives.

---

[31] See Chapter II.

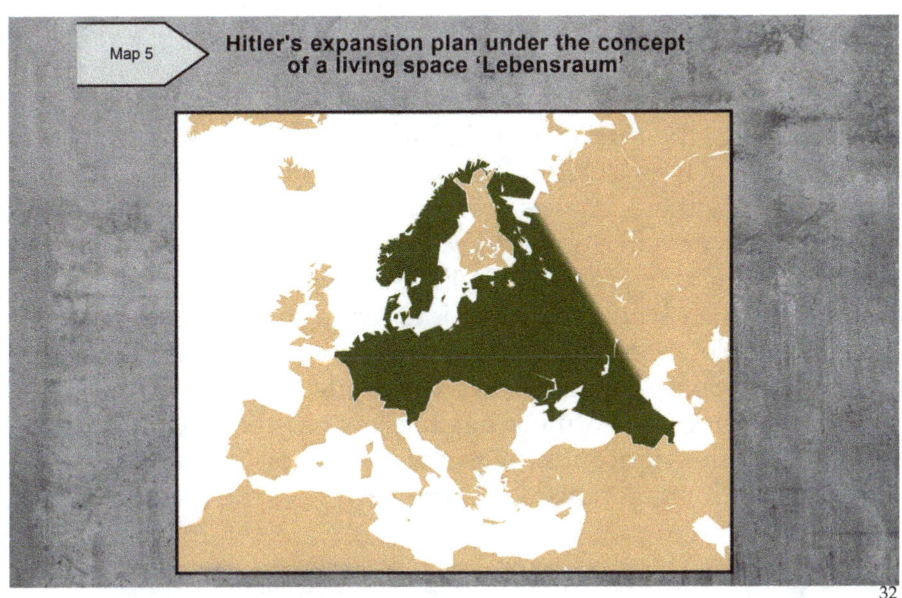

[32]

The above is only a brief mention of some aspects of Hitler's racist views. It is important to understand that these ideologies were not only dangerous, but also caused enormous human suffering and tragedy before and during the Second World War. Hitler's racist beliefs were one of the main factors that led to **genocide and crimes against humanity.**

The Jewish population also lived in other European countries. I will now compare anti-Semitism in Poland and Germany between the wars to show what the situation was like for Jews living in Europe. According to Polish anti-Semitism, one could be an anti-semite and not a racist at the same time. The ideology of Nazism was that anti-Semitism was linked to biological race. The concept of anti-Semitism in the Nazi country was different from its Polish version The source of these differences can be found in the decline of multinational states at the end of the 19th century. 'In the lack of identification of broad sections of society with the institution of the nationalist state; it has also been

---

[32] Map created under the CC BY-SA 3.0 Wikimedia Commons licence, public domain.

noted that the rise of anti-Semitism in Germany took place at a time when Jewish influence in the public sphere was a thing of the past'[33]. Another aspect of the Jewish question was the economic crisis. During the interwar period in Poland and Germany, there were ideas such as isolating the Jewish community from the rest of society. Another idea was to restrict access to schools. There was also the idea of withdrawing Jews from economic and social life and deporting them from the Polish state and from Germany.

In the Polish lands, the most important thing was to treat the Jewish people as culturally alien, unable to assimilate with the Poles. They were also accused of spreading communist ideas. The intensification of resentment against Jews in the interwar period was due to 'the spiritual progress of the nations, which led to the development of nationalism and the decline of the material power of Jewry'[34].

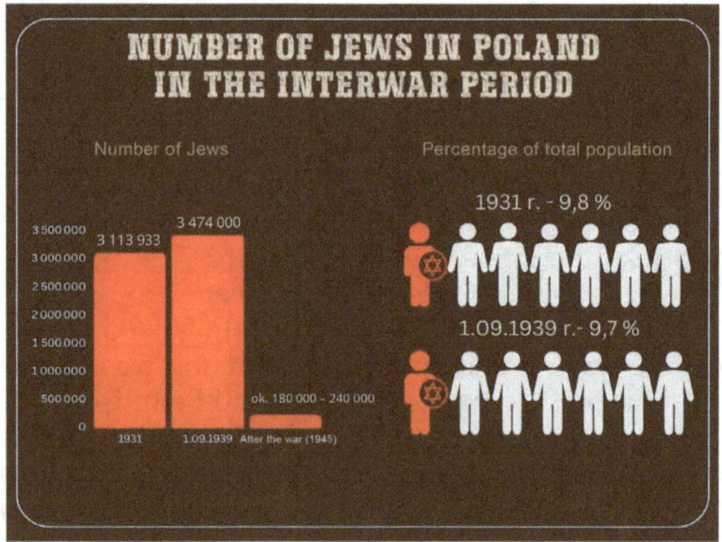

Chart 3. Number of Jews in Poland in the interwar period[35].

---

[33] M. Musielak, *Nazizm w interpretacjach...*, op. cit, pp. 40-41.

[34] Ibidem, pp. 42-43.

[35] Own elaboration based on: http://izrael.badacz.org/zydzi_w_polsce/dzieje_rzeczypospolita.html (accessed 24/09/2023).

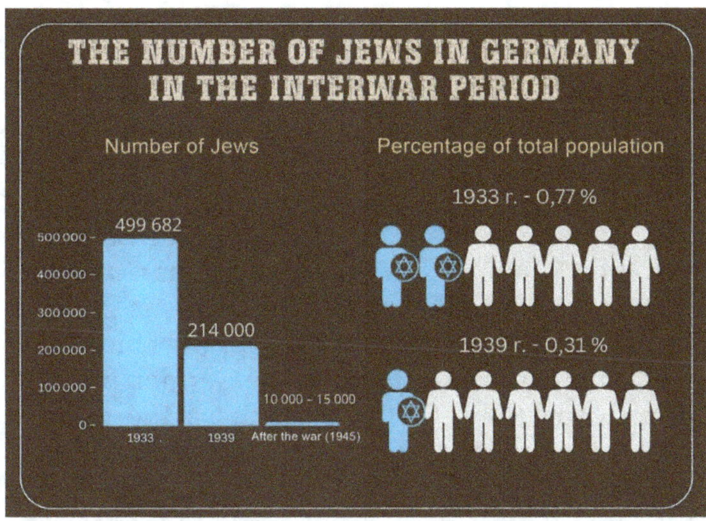

Chart 4. Number of Jews in Germany in the interwar period[36].

As can be seen from the above graphs, the number of Jews in Poland exceeded the number of Jews in Germany in percentage terms. It should be emphasised that in Poland their position in economic, intellectual and cultural life was much lower than in Germany. The situation was similar in other Central and Eastern European countries. Thus, Jewish influence in German banking, industry, medicine, justice, education, literature and politics was considerable. It is worth paying attention to all the crimes against the Jewish population during the reign of Hitler and his policies. If the ideology of 'Lebensraum' was the guiding principle of Nazi policy, then the Jews were not victims of Nazi war policy, because the Jewish people did not inhabit any territories that belonged to them and did not have their own state. The genocide against them therefore had nothing to do with their living space. This is a typical example of the racism of Nazi Germany. An example of Hitler's racial policy was what Heinrich Himmler (a high-ranking Nazi) said to his nation in

---

[36] Own elaboration based on: http://ushmm.org/wlc/en/article.php?ModuleId=10005469 (accessed 24/09/2023).

1936. He declared that: '(...) Germany is only at the beginning of a trial which may last for centuries, perhaps a final trial on a world scale with the organised forces of subhumanity (...)'[37]. Subhuman was to become a universal term for Jews, Roma or Slavs, and for opponents of the Nazis. If one became subhuman, then a 'superhuman' had to be created in contrast. The Nazis identified themselves as superhumans. In the first half of the twentieth century, in the German state, the 'superhuman' was defined as a 'superman', for whom only what he wants is good, and who ruthlessly overthrows everything that opposes him[38].

The Nazis' main idea was to unite the German people through better living conditions. Reforms such as the social security system and the removal of hereditary burdens, the sterilisation policy, made this improvement possible. All this gave German society the moral enthusiasm to believe in the renaissance of the Germanic people. Germans were convinced that these reforms would strengthen them morally and politically, eliminate unemployment, heal economic relations and overturn the Treaty of Versailles, which Germans opposed.

Nazism was the foundation of the new German order. It united the German people and made them proud of their origins. A sense of racial belonging united people in the German state. Racism combined three socio-political attitudes:

- nationalism,
- socialism,
- Prussian – Junker imperialism.

These were contradictory and different attitudes, but in Hitler's mind they worked together. This contributed to his success. 'Nazism was a renaissance of the Germanic offensive against Slavism'[39].

---

[37] A. J. Kamiński, *Hitlerowskie obozy koncentracyjne i hitlerowskie obozy zagłady w polityce imperializmu Niemieckiego*, Poznań 1964, pp. 91-93.

[38] Ibidem.

[39] M. Musielak, *Nazizm w interpretacjach...*, op. cit., p. 34.

German fascism was a natural biological-organic movement, which aimed at:
- *physical and mental health,*
- *the joy of life,*
- *mastery of power, beauty and ugliness,*
- *the harmonious development of individual and social emotions.*

An expression of human needs and aspirations, it refers to primal feelings and instincts.

The difference between Italian and German fascism

The most important difference between German and Italian fascism lay in how racial issues were understood.Whereas in Italy this problem was rather neglected, in German fascism views on racial inequality became a dangerous obsession.

There was also a difference in using terror or force. In contrast to Germany, there were no concentration camps in Italy at all and there were fewer political prisoners.

Attitudes to the Church and religion also varied. In Germany, the attitude was anti-clerical and anti-religious. In Italy, on the other hand, the fascists looked to the Church for support (the head of the Catholic Church, the Pope, is permanently based in the Vatican, i.e. in Italy).

Fascism's guiding idea is nationalism. The most valuable thing for a community is a nation. In the case of the Italian fascists, it was a valuable and cohesive community. Unlike the Italians, the Nazis recognised nationalism as the blood bond that kept the German people together. It was an element of racial purity. The Germans, in their fascist view, did not accept foreign nations. They also saw them as enemies to be destroyed. The main enemies of the German fascists were the Jewish nationality, the Gypsies and the Slavs. Over time, this hostility manifested itself in the harshest and most brutal forms of fighting. Pacifists, intellectuals and communists who opposed fascism were eliminated. The Aryan race was above other races in the Nazi mind. The Aryans were to rule the whole world. Racial views also shaped later occupation policies, which ultimately led to the Holocaust.

Action was taken against representatives of Jewish cultural policy. Contemporary art and jazz, which originated in the United States, were rejected in favour of promoting Nazi ideology. According to this worldview, art should glorify the nation, the heroism of 'superhumans' and traditional family values. The Nazis introduced a series of laws, such as the Nuremberg Laws, which outlawed marriages and sexual relations between native Germans and people of other races, as a desecration of the Aryan race. The subsequent practice of euthanasia and sterilisation was intended to 'improve' the biological value of German citizens, and eugenic practices such as child kidnapping and the idea of 'Lebensborn' were intended to promote the reproduction of future generations according to Nazi racial criteria. Such techniques were not used in Italy. The Nazis were interested in scientific proof of the German people's superiority over others on a biological level, while the Italian fascists focused mainly on armed domination. In the context of the extermination of the subjugated population, the Italians were much less active and on a smaller scale.

Nazism as a totalitarian system

The term 'totalitarianism' originated in Italy in the 1920s. It was used by the philosopher Giovanni Gentileg and the founder of fascism, Benito Mussolini. In other countries, the term was used by philosophers and publicists from 1928. Scholars analysed the different political systems that emerged in Europe after the First World War. Totalitarianism was a response to the crisis of liberal (democratic) state systems and extreme political and ideological orientations. Unfortunately, there is no common definition of totalitarianism that would be accepted by the representatives of European political thought. The elements of totalitarianism are:

- **Mono-partism** - one-party system, where one political party dominates and exercises near-total control over political life, government and state institutions. In Nazi Germany, all key areas, including legislation, the armed forces, the police and the judiciary, were controlled by a single party, the NSDAP. In a one-party system, there is no official and effective party competition, which in practice means that there is no viable alternative to the ruling party. Once in power, the Nazis eliminated all opposition.
- **Media control and propaganda.** In a totalitarian state, the ruling party controls the media, which enables it to control public opinion. In the Nazi state, a Ministry of Propaganda was set up, headed by Joseph Goebbels, another of Hitler's senior men. This ministry had extensive powers to control the media and propagate Nazi ideas. Goebbels had control over broadcasting, the press, film, theatre and even the arts. Strict censorship of media content was introduced under his rule. The Reich Press Chancellery operated to control the content of the press. Immediately after the Nazi seizure of power, the concept of Gleichschaltung was put into practice. The media had to follow an imposed policy and promote the uniform values of Nazi ideology, while journalists had to follow guidelines and avoid content that contradicted the official political line. All other points of view were forbidden, and the media were obliged to promote only national values. Journalists who did not conform to these guidelines were removed from the profession or repressed for excessive journalistic rebellion. Radio and the press, which were particularly significant propaganda tools, were under strict control. The Reichs-Rundfunk Gesellschaft (RRG), the national German radio network, was used mainly for propaganda purposes after 1933. Independent publishers were forced to sell new Nazi publications. On the other hand, media sympathetic to the regime were favoured. They were

granted licences, permits and large sums of money. The film industry was also under state control. Every new film had to be approved by the Ministry of Propaganda, which ensured that films conformed to the imposed ideology. In this way, the Third Reich controlled the media. This allowed the Nazis to effectively manage media broadcasts and shape public opinion according to their own interests and ideology.

• **A leader and a cult of personality** (a leader: 'Führer' in Germany, 'Duce' in Italy). A leader had unquestionable social authority. The commander-in-chief enjoyed full executive and decision-making powers. He was the supreme authority and all major political, military and administrative decisions were taken by him personally. Unlike contemporary democratic systems, where power is usually divided between institutions (e.g. executive, legislature, judiciary), the commander-in-chief enjoyed concentrated power and his decisions were not subject to significant scrutiny. In cultural and political terms, Adolf Hitler was regarded as an undisputed leader and an exceptional human being, and the cult of his person was based on an almost unconditional loyalty to him. As a leader, he influenced many different areas of social, economic, cultural and military life.

• **Corporatism** referred to a model for the organisation of society and the economy in interwar totalitarian states such as the Third Reich. The idea of corporatism, which originated in fascist doctrine, aimed to replace traditional forms of social organisation, such as independent political parties or trade unions, with new structures based on the cooperation of different social groups under state control. Different social groups (employers, workers, farmers, craftsmen, etc.) or even professional associations were united under a single structure. The aim was to create a sense of national community and reduce social conflict. In post-1933 Germany, corporatism manifested itself in intensive planning for the development of the economy, with the state having a decisive influence on these changes.

• **Hierarchy.** The hierarchy in the Third Reich was not only party-based, but also social and militaristic. The country was highly structured. Everything was based on strict subordination to the central authority. The highest authority in the hierarchy was the leader, Adolf Hitler, who served as Führer and Reich Chancellor. Hitler not only exercised political power, but also acted as the chief ideologue and symbol of national unity. The next key position in the hierarchy was held by the National Socialist German Workers' Party (NSDAP), the only legal political party in the Third Reich. People associated with the party enjoyed its high status and membership conferred many privileges. State institutions, such as the Reichstag, were severely restricted and had no influence on major political decisions. The government consisted of ministers whose position was strictly dependent on the will of the Führer.

• **Discipline.** Discipline in the Nazi state was used to control society, eliminate potential opponents and shape society according to the state's ideology. Violence, repression and pervasive control were integral parts of the totalitarian state machine. In 1933, the Gestapo secret police was created to control society. It operated with impunity, using brutality against those suspected of violating ideological values. The submission to the Führer was an absolute necessity in the Wehrmacht. Soldiers swore an oath of loyalty to Hitler. Commanders had extensive disciplinary powers. Schools and the entire education system were also disciplined and controlled by state authorities. Teachers had to accept an ideology and follow the curriculum filled with elements of Nazi propaganda. Young people were subjected to intensive indoctrination by the Hitler Youth (Hitlerjugend), which shaped future citizens in the spirit of Nazi ideology.

In 1937-38, nationalists in neighbouring countries recognised the Third Reich as the state with the most perfect totalitarian system. That is, one 'in which the government itself, animated by great ideas, directs the life of the nation towards its great tasks (...) in accordance with the geopolitical conditions of its being'[40].

The Third Reich created the modern system at a time when there

---

[40] T. Dworak, *Totalne państwo narodowe, Myśl Narodowa* no. 7 of 14/11/1937.

was fascism in Italy and communism in Russia. By terrorising, national socialism managed to unite the young and to bring the different ethnic groups together. It created German morals and customs. Concepts of the German totalitarian system:

- to purify the state of the Jewish people,
- the conquest of the Rhineland (after the First World War this region was demilitarised and not controlled by the German state),
- to reduce unemployment (to fight the Great Depression),
- arming the state and not accepting the Treaty of Versailles.

Photo 3. Lider Adolf Hitler in 1938.

The concept of living space

Let's return to the concept of living space. If we look at the medieval history of the Germanic tribes, we can see that Hitler's policies revived the former predatory possessiveness of Germany. The Führer's rule recalled the Prussian Hohenzollern dynasty and the Teutonic Order, whose main aim was to conquere new lands. The Germans made no secret of their desire for territorial conquest. To do this, they forced Europe to submit to their actions. This was due to the high birth rate in Germany at the turn of the 20th century. Between 1860 and 1910, the population of Germany increased from 37.6 million to 64.6 million people!

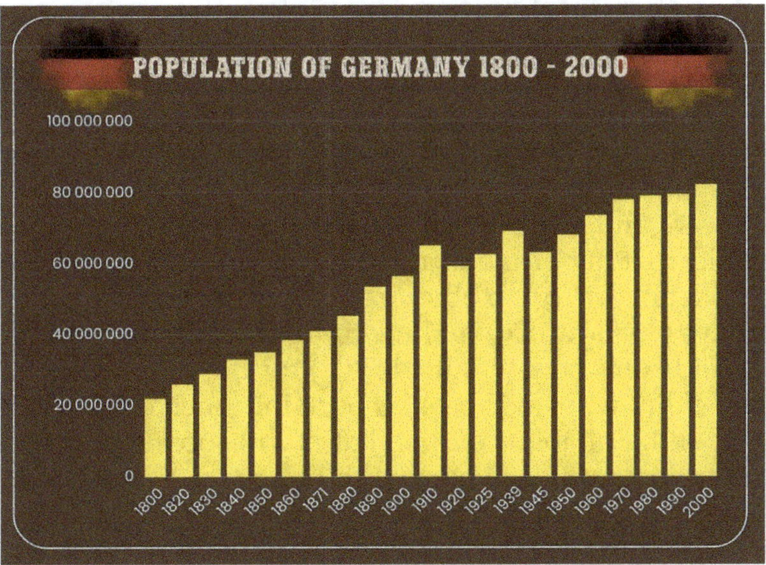

Chart 5. Population of Germany 1800 - 2000[41].

The imperialism of the German state has always been based on a vision of conquest. In the interwar period, therefore, the public was told that the country was overpopulated and needed more living space. As early as the beginning of the 19th century, German aristocrats and writers proclaimed population growth as a national priority. 'When the Hohenlloren baptise a seventh child, they do so as military rulers. So that we can give sons to the

---

[41] Own compilation based on: http://commons.wikimedia.org/wiki/File:Entwicklung_der_Einwohnerzahlen_in_Deutschland.JPG (accessed 09/11/2023).

war! In modern war, the masses decide'[42]. 'Either we reproduce as in the last generation, or we must give up the struggle with the Anglo-Saxons for a decisive share in the external and internal shaping of the world of culture'[43] The society was made to believe that there was an alleged lack of living space, especially after Germany's defeat in the First World War. German writers played a major role in this. For example, Hans Grimm, author of the novel Volk ohne Raum, published in 1926 (during the Second World War more than six thousand copies of the book were printed), wrote in this context 'On a square of one thousand metres, in Germany today, if you mentally separate everything, forest and wilderness and estates and swamps and lakes and rivers, one hundred and thirty-two people must live, and they still want to have houses and factories and stables and cattle and storks and flowers and trees and roads between them. And for every new child that is born, and no one else dies for it, you have to squeeze again (...) for no other nation has ever had so little space as we have (...) How do you think things will go on if you have no space inside and no law outside? (...) for this is the law, that the German child, when it is born, is born into such narrowness that it will soon be unable to cope, that it will soon have to become quarrelsome, that if it is born with the traits of boldness out of sheer necessity, it will be pushed into the wrong path'[44].

The question of living space for Germans was often raised by Adolf Hitler. In his speeches and numerous articles, he proclaimed that Germany had always been an overpopulated area. Hitler claimed that territorial satisfaction could be achieved by acquiring territory in the eastern countries. His main concern was the Poles, who had to be removed quickly. In his speeches before and after coming to power, the same points were made. The German propaganda spread as quickly as

---

[42] T. Dworak, *Totalne...* op. cit., p. 74.

[43] Ibidem.

[44] H. Grimm, *Volk ohne Raum*, Műnchen 1926.

new territory was conquered. Even after conquering new lands, he never stopped saying that Germany did not have enough living space. He declared **war on the United States** in late 1941. He pointed out that the US had 15 people per square kilometre compared to 140 in Germany.

Both the German and the Italian fascists believed that the only way they could build their empires was through war. The Italian fascists differed from the German fascists in that they wanted an empire, whereas the German fascists wanted to create a space for themselves - a 'Raum'. Hitler wrote in *Mein Kampf* that in less than a hundred years there would be 250 million Germans living on the European continent, earning their living through creative work. Over time, the Germans had to deal with new problems caused by the population living in the areas they wanted to conquer.

Population policy and attitudes towards homosexuality

Top Nazis claimed that an increase in the birth rate of German citizens would replace those who died on the battlefield. They argued that it was necessary to multiply in order to have sufficient manpower to conquer the new areas – lands, where the expanding society could settle. The Führer's chief collaborator Heinrich Himmler, making his speeches in 1940 and in 1943, pointed out that it was necessary to create excellent conditions for German families to have many children. He also claimed that families must have many children, so that each generation, could send two or three sons to the army, and at the same time not disturb the rising birth rate. SS officers who were unmarried and over the age of 30 were given instructions and a deadline by Himmler as to when to marry. Otherwise, they had no chance of professional promotion. For higher promotions, the number of children was a determining factor for SS officers[45].

---

[45] Collective work, *Autobiografia Rudolfa Hössa, Komendanta obozu oświęcimskiego*, translated by W. Grzymski, Warszawa 1989.

Photo 4. Heinrich Himmler[46]

HEINRICH HIMMLER - SS commander. He was one of the most influential men in Nazi Germany until the end of the Second World War. The German secret police, security police and criminal police all reported to him. He was responsible for creating and carrying out the 'final solution of the Jewish question'. He oversaw and controlled the Nazi concentration camp system, ation.

In July 1942, an announcement was made that benefits would be issued to Dutch and Norwegian mothers whose children had been begotten by Wehrmacht men[47]. The commander in chief signed an order to multiply the German nation to unrealistic proportions. His intention was to exterminate other nations.

This is how the fundamental problem of the population question is perceived in the ideology of hitlerism.

---

[46] Photo Bundesarchiv, Bild 183-R99621, CC-BY-SA 3.0.

[47] Ibidem.

H. Himmler claimed that in the opinion of some homosexuals, what they do is their private life and the state should not interfere with it. In time, he stated that: 'sex life is no longer a private matter because it concerns the survival of the nation, and therefore we must all understand that we cannot allow this disease to develop in Germany and must fight it ... It is very important that we exterminate them, not out of revenge, but out of necessity of life'[48].

In 1871, a new penal code was introduced on German territory. Paragraph 175 discriminated against the homosexual minority, which had already been discriminated against by the Napoleonic Code. According to this paragraph, sexual intercourse between two men or between a man and an animal should be punished by imprisonment and even loss of civil rights. The prison sentence at the time was two years. This paragraph did not apply to lesbians, as only relations between men were considered morally harmful. Germany was not the only country that had a restrictive attitude towards homosexuals. In other countries, homosexuals were punished by the death penalty.

The definition of homosexuality was introduced two years before paragraph 175 was created. The definition was invented by the Hungarian writer Karl - Maria Kertbeny, who used the word for the first time in his work written anonymously in 1869. He wanted 'to find a neutral and non-offensive term to replace the uranism, omogeny, androtropy, pederasty or sodomy most commonly used at the time'[49]. He is also the author of words such as bisexuality and normasexuality. The term homosexuality came into use very late, more precisely in the 1920s.

Germany was liberal until the 1920s, and although there was the possibility of punishing homosexuals, there was moral freedom in some cities. There were all sorts of clubs, dance halls, bars, same-sex 'friendship leagues' in Berlin and Hamburg.

---

[48] https://racjonalista.pl/kk.php/s,4902 (accessed 16/11/2023).

[49] H. Himmler, Speech to SS lieutenants, 1937 [in:] https://liberte.pl/agnieszka-zakrzewicz-paragraf-175-i-homoseksualizm-wedlug-himmlera/ (accessed 20/11/2023).

Erotic magazines for homosexuals were also available. More and more homosexual literature was also appearing. The role of homosexuals in the Nazi regime was minor, with few individuals engaging in anything. These individuals were only tolerated for specific systemic purposes until threatened, then they were eliminated. Himmler claimed that homosexuals threatened the Aryan race because they were unproductive. Hitler feared that homosexual people could create a state within a state, meaning that they could also enter the political elite. He also feared that they were prone to insubordination and disobedience because of their sexual difference.

The persecution of homosexuals began with Hitler's rise to power in mid-1933. They began to be deprived of their freedom by closing down their bars and clubs, selling homosexual literature was banned and public harassment began. In Berlin, one of the most famous clubs, the 'Eldorado', which hosted all sorts of transsexual performances, was closed down. Homosexuals were called anti-social parasites and idle enemies of the state.

In 1935, amendments were made to paragraph 175, more specifically to the section on 'indecency between men'[50]. This indecency included any behaviour with sexual overtones. Previously, it applied only to sexual intercourse. The number of arrests of gay men in the Third Reich increased tenfold. Preventive arrest was introduced and citizens began to be persuaded to report their gay neighbours. In 1937, a new institution, The Reich Central Office for the Combating of Homosexuality and Abortion, was established. During Himmler's time as chief of police, some 80.000 people were arrested and charged under Section 175. In his speeches, Himmler pointed that since the Nazi had been in power a homosexual organisation with two million members had been exposed. It later turned out that there were many more, not two, but as many as four milions. 'If I assume that there are one and two million homosexuals in this land, it means that 7,

---

[50] J. Hanc, *Homoseksualizm a prawo karne. Analiza synoptyczna*, [in:] *Czasopismo Prawno-Historyczne*, 73(1), Katowice 2021, p. 360.

8 or even 10 percent of German men are homosexual'[51]. He said that if this does not change, the German nation will be destroyed by homosexuality. This will cause a great imbalance of sexuality within this country. He also reffered to the First World War, in which two million German men died, resulting in destabilising the demographic economy in the German nation.

Paragraph 175 defined homosexuality as something against nature and led to discrimination and persecution of the homosexual minority. The German Nazis tried to eliminate gays. The paragraph was still in force for a long time after the war's end, in the German Democratic Republic - until 1967, and in the Federal Republic of Germany - until 1969[52]. Thus, criminal consequences affected homosexuals worldwide from the Middle Ages to the second half of the 20th century.

The concept of slavery and the degeneration of humanity

Another concept of imperialist Nazi Germany was the so-called 'inferior race'. The idea was that other peoples, and above all the peoples of Eastern Europe, could only have the right to exist as Germans' slaves, working for them under inhumane conditions. There was a very thin line between slavery and extermination for the Nazis. At the time of his greatest victories, Hitler used to say that the new territorial conquests and the incorporation of foreign cheap labour were bringing such profits to the Third Reich that the expenses arising from the warfare were not a problem for the state. An instruction from the Minister of the Occupied Eastern Territories, Alfred Rosenberg, stated: 'The Slavs are to work for us. Unless we need

---

[51] H. Himmler, Speech to SS lieutenants, 1937 [in:] https://liberte.pl/agnieszka-zakrzewicz-paragraf-175-i-homoseksualizm-wedlug-himmlera/ (accessed 20/11/2023).

[52] B. Piętka, *Więźniowie z różowym trójkątem w KL Auschwitz* [in:] *Dzieje najnowsze, rocznik XLVI*, Oświęcim 2014. p. 31.

them, they can die out'[53]. Within six years, the need for slaves conflicted with the idea of mass murder of foreign populations. A. Rosenberg wrote that the Germanic tribes initiated a new form of custom in Western Europe at the beginning of our era. He used to say that the Germans were the rulers above other races. In his memorial, H. Himmler referred to the Polish population (Generalgouvernement) and the population related to the Polish nation, the Sorbs. He planned the extermination of the intellectual elite of the eastern lands. Regarding the rest of the population, he said: 'This population will be available as a leaderless working class and will provide the Germans with labourers for special work (roads, quarries, building sites) every year. They will have better living conditions than under Polish rule, and because they will be deprived of their own national identity, under the strict, consistent leadership of the German nation they will be called upon to cooperate in its everlasting cultural projects...'[54].

He also wanted the Polish children to learn simple counting up to 500, to write their surnames and to learn that it was a commandment of God to obey the Germans, to be honest, industrious and noble. As for reading, he did not consider it necessary[55].

This was Himmler's plan for primary schools for the Polish population. We can now see that such a plan led to nothing more than the creation of obedient and dependent slave nations, devoid of their own culture, uneducated and without the natural right to acquire knowledge. Through cruel violence and intimidation, the Nazis intended to create millions of slave-like beings, needed only for primitive manual labour. What is surprising, however, is that in the twentieth century, the need

---

[53] A. J. Kamiński, *Hitlerowskie obozy koncentracyjne...*, op. cit., pp. 112-113.

[54] J. Eisler, M. Sobańska-Bondaruk, *Historia 1789–1990. A selection of source texts for secondary schools*, Warszawa 1995, pp. 197-199.

[55] Ibidem.

for such uneducated labourers passed with the result Himmler dreamed of - the Great Reich. Half a century after the Industrial Revolution, there was a growing need for skilled workers to operate cranes, excavators and other machinery. So why did the Nazis need masses of unskilled slaves? Probably not because of economic conditions, but because the dumber the workers, the less likely they were to revolt.

The commandant of the German concentration camp at Auschwitz-Birkenau from 1940 to 1943, Rudolf Hoess, as a high-ranking SS man, claimed that natural human reflexes were to betray the Führer. The Nazis had to avoid signs of human emotion. Yes, there were individual cases of showing 'mercy' to a fellow human being. There was, for example, the story of Oskar Schindler, a German industrialist who employed Jews in his factory, saving them from deportation and death in the death camps. His actions ultimately saved hundreds of Jews. Another person who acted against the Nazi system during the Second World War was Friedrich Kellner, a German civil servant, a member of the NSDAP in the prewar period, who became an opponent of the Nazi regime during the war. In 1940, Kellner began keeping a diary in which he documented his observations about the actions of the Nazis. He criticised Hitler's regime and condemned the war crimes and cruelty committed by the Nazis. Despite risking being arrested, he kept his diary until the end of the war. After Germany surrendered, his diary was discovered and published. This helped to document the history of the period, revealing many atrocities and war crimes. But these were isolated incidents. Most Nazis were devoid of human feeling. A prime example is the SS man Felix Landau, who took part in the executions of the Lvov professors, among others. He descibed in his notes the execution of 23 Soviet citizens.

He wrote that he felt no pity or emotion at all, a complete 'nothing'. Even his personal story from 1934, when he himself could have been executed during the Vienna putsch, did not help him in his lack of human impulses. At the time, however, the Austrian fascists were lenient towards him and other Nazis[56]. It can be suggested that the Nazis took their cue from the Japanese, who prepared for war by not tolerating the slightest sign of weakness and by ruthlessly suppressing every human reflex in their own soldiers.

The crimes committed by the SS were in the nature of inhuman treatment of another human being, and the term 'inhuman' seems too mild in this context. It is a conventional term. We can speak of perfect examples of dehumanisation when we look at the crimes committed by the Nazis. The signs of immoral behaviour towards people in the concentration camps must also be mentioned. Human skulls and skins were turned into useful objects for industrial purposes. The Nazis used the hair of women murdered in the camps. Sixty tonnes of hair from women gassed in the gas chambers were transported from Auschwitz. It may seem unbelievable that in Buchenwald, the head of the camp's detention centre, Martin Sommer, placed the bodies of murdered prisoners under a couch and then lay down on the couch to sleep[57]. In summary, Nazi ideology is a lack of empathy and compassion for pain. It is hatred of the other.

The concept of eugenics.
Elimination of weak individuals - history

Eugenics is a complex concept. The main premise of eugenics was the improvement of the species from one generation to the next, particularly in terms of inherited traits. Concepts of human improvement in a global sense have existed since the dawn of time. In ancient Sparta, for example, newborn babies with defects were killed. Such practices eliminated weak individuals from Spartan society. It was believed that only healthy and strong individuals had the right to exist in the world.

---

[56] Z. A. Albert, *Kaźń profesorów lwowskich – lipiec 1941*, Wrocław 1989, p. 38.

[57] https://web.archive.org/web/20091005020549/http://www.time.com/time/magazine/article/0,9171,868574,00.html (accessed 20/11/2023).

> **EUGENICS** (from Greek: well-born) is a set of views and methods aimed at improving the condition of the human species, both in terms of biology, psychological traits and morality[58].

> **STERILISATION** (infertility) - irreversible or almost irreversible removal of reproductive capacity by a procedure/ surgery that results in a permanent reduction in fertility[59].

The origins of sterilisation can be found in the procreative practices of societies, as well as in the directives of thinkers and writers throughout the ages.

In modern times[60], it is seen as a product of the evolution of science. The first people to think about sterilisation were primitive people. In those days, the strongest and cleverest came to power, and it was known that this was accompanied by natural selection - very harsh and ruthless. Intuitively, they knew that only strong organisms had a chance of survival. Disabled people were a burden on the rest of society, which struggled to survive from day to day. So, over the years, there has been an effort to eliminate the weak and sick to keep them from becoming burdens on others. This elimination began with the birth of a child. Infanticide and the abandonment of children were practised mainly by 'uncivilised' people. The Indians, for example, were known to sacrifice children to the gods, but also to drown them in rivers. The Carthaginians sacrificed their children also. The Aztecs sacrificed children in honour of the rain god, and in Mingrelia (now Georgia), when there was no means of raising offspring, killing a child was considered

---

[58] source: Encyklopedia PWN (accessed 15/11/2023).

[59] source: Encyklopedia PWN (accessed 15/11/2023).

[60] Modern times – also the modern era, the historical era between 1492 and 1789.

a benevolent act[61]. Among the Aborigines, deformed children were killed immediately after birth. Similar customs existed in many other countries. In some countries, girls were killed because boys would grow up to be hunters. Historically, it was natural to eliminate weak people, sickly and disabled children, and infirm old people. Society had to restrict access to food because it could not afford to carry the burden of the weak, let alone children who were unable to feed and care for themselves. Girls were particularly hard hit, as they were simply not needed in a society that valued physical strength[62].

Plato, from a philosophical point of view, developed the issue of population sterilisation. He believed that the authorities should control the reproduction of society. Those who were useful and deserving among other citizens were chosen to have children. For example, those who fought in wars or served the state. In his ideal state, infanticide was acceptable. He also believed that it was necessary to select married couples in order to produce perfect offspring. Aristotle was also in favour of sterilisation. He believed that it was necessary to abandon handicapped children, but also to abort families with more than the permitted number of children. The above examples could be given in greater numbers.

In modern times, the origins of sterilisation come from the natural sciences. They emerged at the turn of the 18th and 19th centuries. Discoveries about heredity and theories about thedegeneration of the human species influenced the origins of sterilisation. These studies aimed to prove that pathological traits in the human species were passed on from generation to generation, resulting in various degenerations. The study of the human species led to a theory that had as a goal the prevention of the formation of negative traits and the control of human reproduction. The scientist Francis Galton pioneered the

---

[61] M. Musielak, *Sterylizacja ludzi ze względów eugenicznych w Stanach Zjednoczonych, Niemczech i Polsce (1899 - 1945)*, Poznań 2008, p. 20.

[62] Ibidem.

concept that a population should consist only of outstanding individuals. He argued that the more gifted individuals there were in a society, the better a civilisation would be. By analysing the genealogical connections of prominent figures in science, the arts, the military, sport and other prestigious professions, he came to believe that outstanding individuals often inherited not only physical traits, such as hair colour and height, but also mental, emotional and creative qualities, such as a talent for politics, sport or writing[63]. In his view, these qualities are not random, since the offspring of parents with exceptional intelligence also exhibit outstanding abilities. An important date in the history of the concept of eugenics is 1883, when F. Galton first used the term eugenics. The term was used to describe the activities involved in improving a race. It marked a new scientific discipline, aimed at improving paternal heredity and contributing to crossbreeding. Eugenics was concerned with the genetic improvement of human traits in the areas of intelligence, health and morality. In the field of health, for example, modern eugenics was intended to eradicate disease and to increase energy and vitality. These ideas were seen by him as cumulative into a characteristic he called value. This term had reference to the attitude of the citizen.

So much for the history of the concept of eugenics and sterilisation. In the following section, I will focus mainly on the country of Germany before and after Adolf Hitler's rise to power.

Sterilisation in Germany before 1933

Sterilisation in Germany was undoubtedly influenced by the eugenics movement known as racial hygiene. This movement began at the end of the 19th century. The theorist of eugenics in Germany was Alfred Ploetz. He put forward his theory of

---

[63] Ibidem.

the degeneration of modern society through social policy. He believed that protecting the weak would stop the natural selection of people. His concept is summed up in his words: 'The only remedy for this process, which is harmful to mankind, or rather to the race, is the introduction of mechanisms of controlled procreation, whereby persons with valuable qualities would be granted the right to have offspring, while persons of little value would be restricted in the sphere of reproduction'[64]. The concept referred to natural selection, the laws of medicine and biology, which should create the best conditions for the development of the race and society as a whole.

Another practitioner of German eugenics was Wilhelm Schallmayer, who worked with Alfred Ploetz. He described his ideas on eugenics as a science concerned with the danger of physical degeneration of peoples and the hygiene of heredity. In 1905 he used the term 'national biology'. This was followed by the term 'racial hygiene'. There were supporters and critics of this concept among researchers, mainly Germans. The supporters were convinced that society was a hierarchical system with different human races, and at the top of this hierarchy were the Aryan tribes.

For German eugenics theorists, racial hygiene was an objective science based on the elimination of the weak in society. A number of movements emerged in Germany[65]:

• The first trend of racial hygiene, was active until the rise of the Third Reich. At that time, German eugenics was dominated by proponents of the Aryan racial concept. The main proponent of this movement was, among others, the aforementioned Wilhelm Schallmayer. He was the first to specify the theoretical basis of German eugenics. He was inspired by the views of the author of racial hygiene and the zoologist Ernest Haeck, as well as by the assumptions of social Darwinism. From Haeck's ideas he borrowed a critical attitude towards egalitarianism and a belief in

---

[64] M. Musielak, *Sterylizacja ludzi…*, op. cit., p. 155.

[65] I. Sugalska, Eugenika. *W poszukiwaniu istoty niemieckiego totalitaryzmu*, Poznań 2015, p. 190.

the superiority of the interests of the community and the limited role of the individual. In his works, he wrote that a law should be introduced to restrict marriages between people of little value. He also wanted health certificates to be introduced to show who was a strong, healthy, valuable person and who was not. According to him, this would lead to the betterment of the human race.

> **EGALITARIANISM** - a socio-political view that assumes the inherent equality of all human beings and recognises the principle of equality as the basis of a just social system; it is also the aspiration to make all members of society economically and politically equal[66].

• The second movement of racial hygiene was initiated by Alfred Ploetz, who also fought against the degeneration of humanity, but argued for the protection and development of the Nordic race. The movement flourished after the First World War. One of the proponents of this concept was Ernest Rudin. He wanted to limit the reproduction of people with defective hereditary traits. According to him, alcoholics had such traits, and he wanted to isolate them from society. He also advocated their sterilisation if any of them planned to marry. After the First World War, he became involved in research into the genealogy of German families, using sources from church, prison and hospital, as well as interviews. He published his findings in a few journals, earning him the name of a leading German eugenicist.

A. Ploetz's activities developed the eugenics movement in Germany. German journals, to which most of the German public had access, published texts by significant researchers of the time. The texts dealt with evolutionary biology, genetics, health economics and anthropology.

Fritz Lenz, who believed that population policy should be

---

[66] source: Encyklopedia PWN, entry: Egalitaryzm (accessed 15/11/2023).

guided by the principles of Nordicisation and the selection and denial of reproduction of people of little value, had other views on the subject. He preached that Nordics and Jews should come first in the racial hierarchy because they were the most creative races. After a while, however, he changed his mind and preached anti-Semitic views. He specialised in research into the genealogical and serological inheritance of family traits. This research made him an expert in the field. He also recommended people for sterilisation[67].

It was not only researchers in universities and other institutions who were interested in German social policy. Eugenics organisations were also developing the concept. In these organisations, it was no longer new theories that were put forward, but practical action. Steps were taken to save German society from demographic disaster and health problems. Thanks to the activity of members of the German Society for Racial Hygiene, legislative steps were taken in Germany between the wars, and new laws were introduced. These regulations made it possible to develop public health care and to combat venereal diseases and tuberculosis. The new laws also protected the family.

The Third Reich - who did the Nazis want to get rid of and why?

In the Third Reich, health care was an important instrument of social policy. Politicians had different views. Two trends emerged. The racist attitude sought to introduce a policy of 'Aryanisation' - the elimination of people of little value. People were made aware of the restrictions they could face if they did not conform to the principles of eugenic procreation. In 1921, before the Nazis came to power, a Racial Hygiene Committee was set up to draft legislation. It was designed to allow abortion and help large families. They also dealt with the introduction

---

[67] I. Sugalska, *Eugenika*, op. cit., p. 202.

of sterilisation and eugenics education at university level. However, this direction did not find many supporters in those years. This led to the founding of the German League for National Rebirth and Knowledge of Heredity in 1926. The aim of this organisation was to increase public knowledge of eugenics. This was done through press publications, artistic events and propaganda films.

On 14 July 1933, the Law for the Prevention of Hereditarily Diseased Offspring was introduced, implementing the compulsory sterilisation of German citizens. The Nazi authorities considered this to be the most important law of the time. The highest authorities of the Third Reich were anxious to get it passed as quickly as possible, despite many objections from abroad. This determination to introduce castration and sterilisation came from their own views and ideas. They promoted it wherever they could. German officials explained that it would quickly isolate people of little value from German society. By the end of 1933 it was estimated that around 360,000 men and women, including children, would be subjected to this procedure. Approximately 6,500 people died as a result. The authorities drew up a list of medical conditions that qualified for the operation. These included Down's syndrome, hydrocephalus, schizophrenia, depression and other mental disorders, epilepsy, blindness, deafness and alcoholism. The identification of potential victims was the responsibility of medical professionals and teachers, and the decision was made by 181 hereditary health tribunals, all in accordance with the law[68].

Adolf Hitler preached in his book Mein Kampf that a better race should be cleansed of certain foreign elements. He also believed that 'everything clearly diseased and hereditarily burdened should be declared unfit for reproduction, and this principle should be carried out in practice'[69]. Other Nazi Party leaders also shared

---

[68]   Zechenter A., 'Wyhodować niemiecką bestię', IPN Bulletin 1-2/2023.

[69]   A. Hitler, *Mein Kampf*, München 1943, p. 145.

these views. Alfred Rosenberg suggested castration for repeat offenders. The Nazi Richard Walther Darre divided women into four groups. The first two, with good or best hereditary qualities, should be supported by the state. The other two are women with negative characteristics, those with mental illness or those from extramarital relationships. They should be sterilised.

The success of sterilisation in Nazi Germany depended mainly on the organisation and smooth functioning of the health service. It also depended on the introduction of several pieces of legislation that would lead to its implementation. In August 1939, Wilhelm Frick, the head of the Ministry of the Interior, issued a secret order that the births of children deemed 'worthless' should be registered in hospitals using the appropriate forms. These babies were sent to one of forty 'special children's wards' where doctors subjected them to extreme practices or left them to starve to death. It is estimated that between 1939 and 1945 at least 5,000 people were killed in 'children's wards' with the tacit approval of the authorities. Older children with 'defects' or who were considered 'difficult' were sent to asylums where some were deprived of their lives[70].

One of the postulates of the Nazi party NSDAP was the fundamental duty of the citizen, the duty to work, either physically or mentally. The activity of the individual should not interfere with the interests of the rest of society. The individual should serve the common good of all citizens. On this basis, Hitler sought to increase national power by eliminating the mentally ill, including children. He believed that by eliminating some 700,000 to 800,000 of the most vulnerable children each year, he could achieve the desired effect. The Führer knew that it would be difficult to convince the nation to eliminate the mentally ill, so he presented the problem on four different levels[71]:

---

[70] Zechenter A., 'Wyhodować niemiecką bestię', IPN Bulletin 1-2/2023.

[71] E. Sadowska, *Eugenika a bezpieczeństwo jednostki. Historia myśli, rozwój, przyszłość*, Kraków 2018. pp. 136-140.

- the creation of a theory based on the ideology of racial hygiene that would encourage Hitler's leaders to extend eugenic measures to eliminate the mentally ill,
- the introduction of racial laws that would prepare the ground for the legalisation of euthanasia,
- the spread of these theories through intense propaganda to gain public acceptance,
- the creation of a pro-euthanasia group among psychiatrists to develop a treatment plan and transform the psychiatric treatment system.

The Nazis waited until the rest of society agreed to eliminate the mentally ill. After 1933, the Nazi government took control of scientific institutions. It set up departments of racial hygiene in German universities. This led eugenicists to start implementing eugenic reform on their own. One of the leading geneticists responsible for the Nazi crimes was Otto von Verschuer. His essay, The Racial Biology of the Jews, was published in Hamburg in 1938. It was one of 50 articles published in six volumes. This work was published under the German title Forschungen zur Judenfrage [Reflections on the Jewish Question]. His research was supported financially and morally by the national socialist government[72].

The article dealt with the alleged physical differences between Germans and Central European Jews. Verschuer pointed out that the Jewish ethnic group had survived for almost two thousand years without a separate territory. The scholar took great care to give the article a scientific tone. He achieved this, for example, by discussing blood groups, fingerprints and susceptibility to disease. These are all topics appropriate to an anthropologist. The researcher has created a document full of ethnic hatred under the guise of scientific research. In his book we read that Jews have hooked noses, flushed skin with a light tint of yellow, fleshy lips or curly

---

[72] J. Glad, *Eugenika w dwudziestym pierwszym wieku*, 2007, pp. 75-76 [in:] http://whatwemaybe. org/txt/txt0002/Glad.John.2007.FHE.polish.pdf (accessed 22/11/2023).

hair. They are characterised by a strange way of walking and a very specific odour. Verschuer also describes 'pathological racial characteristics'. He does not deny the high intelligence of the Jews or the low birth rate of the Jewish people, but by the end of the article his hatred is sufficiently clear. 'I believe that only people of a certain type are able to sympathise with Judaism and recognise this religion, especially people who feel connected to Judaism by virtue of their intellectual and psychological profile'. (Rarely could these be physical characteristics). In this sense, the element incorporated into the Jewish community was not 'alien'[73].

There is also Verschuer's advice that Jews and Germans must necessarily keep a distance between themselves. This attitude was identical to Hitler's in Mein Kampf, where the Führer states that one of the greatest human rights and duties is to preserve the purity of the blood. Verschuer also lists pregnancy prevention recommendations. He mentions 'syphilitics, tuberculosis sufferers, the genetically handicapped, cripples and idiots'[74]. He writes about preventing 'full-blooded' Germans from interbreeding with other groups. All this to prevent the development of disability and social handicap.

Another social group that the Nazis considered unneeded in their ideal world were the mentally ill. Hitler regarded the patients in psychiatric institutions as 'parasites' who unnecessarily occupied hospital beds and wasted staff time[75]. In September 1939, he secretly issued an order initiating a national euthanasia programme. He issued this order to make available some 80,000 hospital beds. These beds were to be prepared for future war victims. An extreme example of Nazi Germany's eugenics policy was Hitler's 1939 order 'The terminally ill shall be allowed to die with dignity'[76]. This order was to mark the beginning of an action codenamed T4. This action consisted of the killing

---

[73] Ibidem, pp. 76-77.

[74] Ibidem.

[75] Ibidem, p. 84.

[76] A. Rudziewicz, *Eugenika a osiągnięcia współczesnej genetyki*, Warszawa 2005, p. 8.

(mainly by gassing, shooting and injecting poison) of incurably ill people. It is estimated that more than 200,000 patients were exterminated as part of this operation between 1939 and 1945. Those directly responsible for this criminal operation were based at Tiegartenstrasse 4 in Berlin. The operation was named after this address. Internally, the German authorities used terms such as 'Aktion E' or 'Eu', which was an abbreviation of the word 'euthanasia' (Greek for 'good death').

The eugenics movement should not be seen as the cause of the extermination of the Jews. Hitler supported eugenics, but it is not true that his hatred and negative attitude towards the Jewish people came from the views of eugenicists, who supposedly regarded them as intellectually inferior people. On the contrary, Hitler saw the Jews as a powerful rival to the Aryan race, in whom he saw the victors. The Jewish people were blamed for Germany's defeat in the First World War and for the humiliating terms of the Treaty of Versailles. When it became clear that the Germans would have to fight another war, there was a widespread desire for revenge against other races. The Slavs and Gypsies were particularly targeted. The Gypsies were to be exterminated, while the Slavs, as a group of inferior tribes, were to work as slaves for the Germans. The tragic extermination of Gypsies, Jews and many Slavs at the end of the war took place in complete secrecy. German eugenicists did not call for the Holocaust.

Eugenics is not a Holocaust[77] ideology and cannot be blamed for the tragedy of the Second World War. It is a fact, however, that in this one country a small group of its practitioners were complicit in war crimes. The views of eugenicists were not, however, the driving force behind German national socialism, as is commonly reported. Hitler's government used them to justify its actions when it faced opposition from scientists.

---

[77] Holocaust is the term used to describe the extermination of the Jews in Europe by the Third Reich during the Second World War (source: Encyclopedia PWN - accessed 15/11/2023).

Concentration camps and extermination camps

When most people of the living generations hear the words 'concentration camp' or 'extermination camp', the first thing that comes to their minds is Auschwitz-Birkenau (Oświęcim[78]), because it is the most known Nazi camp in the world. When I was at school and we discussed the Holocaust and the cruelty that took place during the Second World War, and the term 'German camp' was mentioned, my first thought was this camp. But the history of the Nazi camps is not only about the town of Auschwitz. Read it if you want to know more.

The origins of the Nazi concentration camps date back to 1933, following Hitler's appointment as Chancellor of the German state[79]. On the basis of a decree issued by the Führer on 28 February of that year, the so-called 'protective custody' (Schutzhaft) was established. These decrees abolished the basic rights guaranteed by the constitution, in particular the personal freedom of German citizens. These laws made it possible to arrest and imprison without trial all opponents of Nazism who were considered enemies of the state. The camps were originally administered by the SA[80], but from June 1934 they came under the control of the SS. The Nazi party, the NSDAP, took over full control of the concentration camps. The creation of the camp system was the result of cooperation between the political apparatus, the administration of the Third Reich, the German monopolies, the police and the Wehrmacht[81].

The first camp of this type was Columbia Haus, founded by the SS and SA in Berlin in February 1933. Other camps of this type were set up in Breslau (a German city between the wars, and now part of Poland), Oranienburg and Emsland (Westphalia). People who were considered enemies of Hitler's

---

[78] Polish name for Auschwitz.

[79] The event took place on 30 January 1933.

[80] Fascist militias.

[81] Wehrmacht - the regular army of the Third Reich.

ideology were sent to these places without being tried. Initially, the camps operated illegally, on the instructions of local SS or SA commanders. By the end of 1933, there were already 55 such places in the Third Reich[82].

Although the German state played a key role in establishing the system of concentration and death camps, it is worth pointing out that this was not an isolated case. In the 19th century, between 1895 and 1898, the Spanish used temporary concentration camps during the Cuban rebellions, imprisoning some 400,000 people (including the elderly, women and children). This was done to terrify the local population and the freedom fighters. In addition to the Spanish, the British also used these practices in South Africa, where some 120,000 people were recruited in 20 camps. The aim was to put pressure on the Boer (Afrikaner) rebels, but the camps were quickly closed following public protests[83].

The first official 'legal' camp was established at Dachau, near Munich. It was established on 22 March 1933, almost two months after Adolf Hitler became Chancellor of Germany. The initiator of the first 'legal' camp was the then SS Chief Commander Heinrich Himmler. In the following years, 1936-1939, concentration camps were mainly used for the elimination of political opponents of the Nazi regime and those suspected of activities harmful to the German state. Gradually, the range of those imprisoned was extended to include other social groups. These included criminals, the homeless, members of religious sects, homosexuals and Jews. Prisoners were placed in camps for an undefined period, and the SS authorities decided what happened to them. During these years, camps such as Sachsenhausen, Buchenwald, Flossenbürg, Mauthausen and Neuengamme were established. It is estimated that 170,000 people were imprisoned in all the camps by 1939[84].

---

[82] http://majdanek.com.pl/obozy/historia%20obozow.html (accessed 18/11/2023).
[83] Ibidem.
[84] N. Widok, *Przeżyć*, Wałbrzych 2018, p. 6.

After the invasion of Poland and the outbreak of the Second World War, the third phase of the construction of concentration camps and mass extermination sites began. From then on, the Germans established camps outside their own territory. From September 1939, existing camps within Germany were expanded and new concentration camps were established in European territories as the areas occupied by the Nazis expanded. In the conquered territories, the Stutthof camp by the sea in Poland was established at the beginning of September 1939. Initially it was a camp for civilian prisoners of war from Pomerania, but over time such places were transformed. From being centres of isolation and forced labour, they became an overarching tool for the biological destruction of conquered peoples. The Nazi camps in Eastern Europe, especially in the Polish lands, were used to eliminate the elites of these countries. The camps were also used to exterminate the Jewish and Slavic populations and to support the German colonisation of these territories, known in history as the 'General Plan East'. The location of the camps was chosen on the basis of a number of factors: convenient transport infrastructure, conditions conducive to hiding traces of the crimes, proximity to the social groups to be exterminated, and proximity to production facilities (e.g. mines or quarries) so that the slave labour of the prisoners could be exploited to the full. In addition, unfavourable climatic conditions, such as swampy areas, were used to devastate the prisoners, as was the case at Auschwitz-Birkenau and Dachau. The Auschwitz-Birkenau camp was established in May 1940 and over time became the largest concentration camp in the occupied territories.

Gradually, throughout occupied Europe, the network of concentration camps expanded.

> Among the largest camps established after the outbreak of war were Stutthof (1939), Auschwitz-Birkenau (1940), Neuengamme (1940), Natzweiler-Struthof (1940), Gross-Rosen (1940), Bergen-Belsen (1940), Majdanek (1941), Chełmno (1941), Treblinka II (1942), Bełżec (1942), Sobibór (1942), Płaszów (1942), 's-Hertogenbosch in the Netherlands (1942), Riga-Kaiserwald (1943), Dora (1943), Amersfoort (Netherlands), Breendonk (Belgium), Faldstadt (Norway), Horseroed (Denmark), Šiauliai, Vilnius and Smolensk (USSR), Theresienstadt (Czech Republic).

The German camps had various specific functions. Types of camps[85]:

• **Extermination camps** - there were four: Treblinka Concentration Camp, Sobibor Concentration Camp, Belzec Concentration Camp, Kulmhof (in Polish: Chełmno nad Nerem) Concentration Camp. I would also include camp in Auschwiz Birkenau among extermination camps from 1942. Such places were used to carry out regular killings. The victims of extermination were mostly Jews and Roma, who were condemned to genocide. The extermination camps were located in forests, in quiet, low populated areas, with access to specially constructed railway sidings. Their sole purpose was the immediate extermination of millions of people. Future victims were brought in by train. Executions were mainly carried out in gas chambers, without prior registration of persons. Very few prisoners worked in such camps, some of whom were selected during the selection process. The prisoners who worked there lived in barracks. Their task was to operate the death machine, i.e. the gas chambers and crematoria. Their duties also included preparing the bodies of the murdered for cremation (cutting hair, removing gold teeth), sorting the victims' clothes and belongings, melting gold into

---

[85] https://zwangsarbeit-archiv.de/pl/zwangsarbeit/erfahrungen/lager/index.html (accessed 20/11/2023).

bars for shipment to the Third Reich Bank, etc;

- **Concentration camps** - were used for imprisonment, isolation, exploitation, humiliation, intimidation, and forced labour. While extermination camps were mainly located in occupied Poland, the majority of concentration camps were located in Germany. Examples of such camps were Dachau Concentration Camp, Sachsenhausen Concentration Camp, Buchenwald Concentration Camp and Ravensbrück Concentration Camp. These were places where political opponents, homosexuals, 'sub-humans' mainly from Eastern Europe, Jehovah's Witnesses, homeless people, criminals, etc. were held. German citizens were also imprisoned in these camps;

- **Subcamps** - were set up mainly in areas of the Third Reich after 1943. They were organised to provide forced labour for the SS, state and private enterprises. There were different categories of these subcamps, ranging from smaller work centres, where support work was organised, to larger ones, which dealt with the disarming of unexploded bombs, repair work, etc., to military factories and the most severe subcamps associated with underground construction;

- **The educational labour camps** - were a type of 'short stay' concentration camp used to discipline unruly citizens, mainly those who refused to work for the state. Later, foreigners were also sent there for forced labour. These camps were set up by the local police - the Gestapo. The total number of such camps is estimated at 200;

- **Prisoner of War Camps (POW camps)** - were set up and run by the Wehrmacht. As well as transit camps near the front, there were oflags (camps for officers) and stalags (camps for ordinary soldiers). Prisoners of war were forcibly taken to work in specific sectors of the economy (mainly industry, agriculture and forestry). The camps also took a human toll. More than three million Soviet war prisoners were sentenced to death by starvation during the war, and almost two million soldiers of various nationalities were forced to work for the German war economy;

- **Camps for children and young people** - were located in the occupied Polish territories, for example in Łódź and in Potulice. These were a separate type of camps. Children were imprisoned in all Nazi camps, but those classified as suitable for Germanisation[86] were sent to special Germanisation camps, from where they were handed over to German families in the Third Reich;

• **Ghettos** - places of isolation, exploitation and death for the Jewish population. In more than 600 cities (e.g. Łódź, Warsaw, Riga) about four million Jews were brought together. They were sent to concentration camps and death camps. At the end of the hostilities and with the withdrawal of the German army, these places were cleared out and the entire population living there was, for the most part, sentenced to death. It is estimated that around 700,000 people died in the ghettos[87].

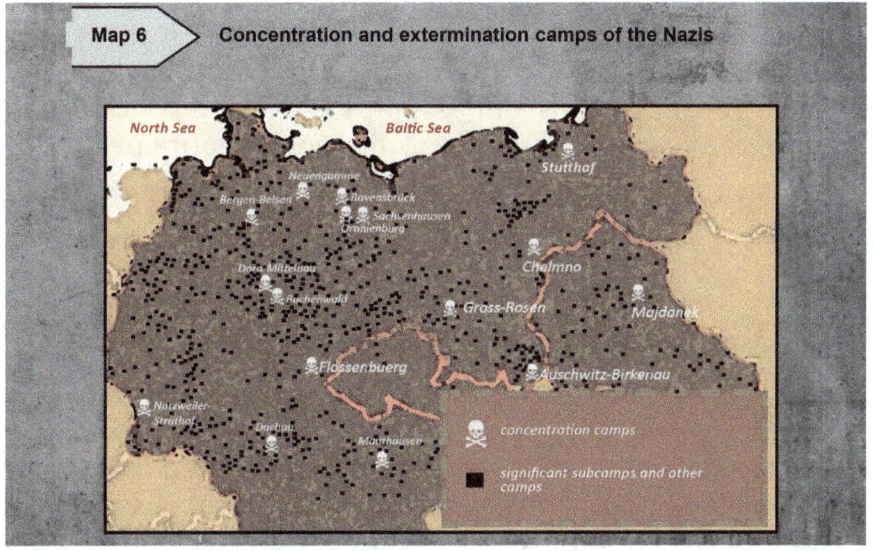

[88]

The camp system was extremely well-organised. Particular attention was paid to the prevention of escape attempts. Care was taken to ensure the proper selection of personnel, the use

---

[86] Germanisation - imposing or assimilating German culture and language.

[87] http://izrael.badacz.org/historia/szoa_obozy.html (accessed 18/11/2023).

[88] Own map based on source: http://izrael.badacz.org/galeria/camp.html (accessed 20/11/2023).

of technical measures for security or terror, the construction of bunkers, and the proper and efficient functioning of the gas chambers and crematoria. Each camp was headed by a commandant who was responsible only to the central SS authorities. He was assisted by the commandant, the staff and the prison administration of the camp. There was a Gestapo office in each camp to supervise the prisoners, to deal with particularly dangerous individuals, to uncover acts of resistance and to track down saboteurs.

For the prisoners, life in the camp usually ended tragically. They died of starvation (the food ration in Auschwitz, for example, was only 700 calories a day[89]), brutal beatings, torture or infectious diseases (typhus, tuberculosis, dysentery). The sick, elderly and disabled were eliminated by injections of phenol. But even in such a terrible situation, the prisoners did not lose hope of survival. In 1941, the construction of gas chambers for the mass murder of the population began. The concentration camps became a tool for the extermination of entire peoples.

> In January 1942, at a meeting in Wansee, the Nazi leaders decided to implement a plan for the 'final solution of the Jewish question in Europe', which involved the extermination of all Jews living in Europe.

In the camps, people were murdered with phenol and benzine injections or with Zyklon-B in the gas chambers, and their bodies burned at the stake, in crematoria or buried in lime pits. In the final stages of the war, the Germans set about removing all traces of their crimes. The camps were decommissioned and everything that reminded people of the cruelty there was destroyed. From January 1945, several thousand prisoners were shot or died of cold and exhaustion during the evacuations known as 'death marches' (forced evacuations). Hundreds of thousands of prisoners were evacuated to concentration camps

---

[89] https://auschwitz.org/historia (accessed 18/11/2023).

in Germany to complete the work of extermination (Hitler believed he would win the war).

In all, the Nazis organised 12,000 different camps and subcamps throughout the Third Reich and its 17 occupied and dependent states. Some 18 million people were imprisoned in all the camps, 11 million of whom died. Concentration and extermination camps held a total of about 9 million people, of whom at least 7.2 million died tragically[90]. This means that 81% of all prisoners died. The exact number of inmates and victims of the Nazi camps is difficult to determine because the Nazis succeeded in erasing most traces of their crimes. Responsibility for the genocide committed in the Nazi camps lies with the authorities of the Third Reich, the Nazi criminals, the criminal Nazi organisations such as the NSDAP, the Gestapo, the SS, the SA, the Wehrmacht, the German judicial authorities of the time, the propaganda authorities and the scientific institutions.

In summary, the system of labour, concentration and extermination camps was developed on a large scale and included a variety of functions. They ranged from forced labour camps to places of mass murder. The camps were efficiently run. There were safeguards against escape, careful selection of personnel, adequate security measures, the construction of gas chambers and crematoria. The people there suffered degradation, humiliation and injustice.

Dear reader, I hope that I gave you a brief account of the ideology responsible for the tragedy of millions of people during the Second World War. History books tend to be voluminous and written in difficult language, incomprehensible to the average reader. It makes people reluctant to learn about history. I hope you enjoyed reading this and that you understand everything I say. I believe that if you have read the previous chapter, you will already know what Europe and the rest of the world looked like in the period from 1918 to 1945. I invite you to the next chapter, where

---

[90] http://majdanek.com.pl/obozy/historia%20obozow.html (accessed 18/11/2023).

I will continue to talk about concentration and death camps, and specifically take you into the world of pseudo-medicine. I will show you what medical experiments were like in the Nazi camps.

In 1942, SS doctors began carrying out intensive medical (pseudo-medical) experiments in the camps. These included testing the human body's ability to withstand changing weather conditions, testing new drugs, deliberately infecting people with malaria, typhus, purulent infection, tuberculosis, transplanting muscle and bone fragments, sterilisation, castration or freezing. The results of these experiments were to be used by German chemical and pharmaceutical companies and by the Wehrmacht. The research resulted in serious illness, disability or death. You will read all about this in Chapter II. But first I want to mention the psychological side.

Why did the Germans believe it?
Social psychology

I always wondered how ordinary Germans could have embraced Adolf Hitler's ideology. Blindly obsessed with one person, they lost their human reflexes, their emotions and their sense of empathy for others. Imagine someone in a civilised European country today acting that way. Imagine someone who openly advocates hatred, violence and murdering nations to make his own state bigger. Today, we would probably search for that person on social media, write a comment like 'you are sick' or something similar, and report the matter to the relevant law enforcement authorities. Such a person would go to jail for inciting hatred and the case would probably be closed. At least that is the way I see it. How is it possible for the radical forces of the Nazi Party to gain such popular support in a democratic, civilised state? Adolf Hitler did not come to power by Putsch but by democratic election. Were the German people unaware of the consequences of the Nazi Party's actions? This is where we need to go back to 1919 and the provisions of the Versailles Treaty.

The loss of an empire and the humiliating terms of the treaty that ended the First World War for the Germans had made the public want to know more about the Nazi agenda. One of the Nazis' key points was to criticise the terms of the treaty, which were seen as damaging and humiliating for Germany. From the very beginning of his political activity, Adolf Hitler advocated the rejection of this document, the immediate abolition of the payment of reparations and an unwillingness to compromise. (See above to find more about 19th century German imperialism). The German people felt a sense of lost imperial power. At the time of the German Empire, Germany was admired and respected on the international stage. It had a powerful army, capable of defending itself effectively and conducting major military campaigns. The terms of the Treaty of Versailles were an insult to German national honour.

The turning point in Germany was the Great Depression that shook the world. For many years before the crisis, Nazi slogans were unpopular with the people. Between 1924 and 1929, the German people enjoyed stability and a good life. It was only when the world was plunged into crisis that this apparent stability was shattered. The economic system of the German state, built on fragile postwar foundations, proved extremely vulnerable to shocks. The need to repay high compensation became a huge burden for a weakening economy faced with growing debt. Unemployment quickly rose to over 40%. In one of the richest countries in Europe, more than a third of the population suddenly found themselves living in poverty. The crisis led to social divisions and pessimism turned to supporting radical political solutions. **There must always be someone to blame**, so the blame for the crisis was put on the Jews, the communists, the bankers and the western states. The charismatic Hitler used the current public mood to his advantage. He was an excellent speechmaker who could adapt his speeches to different social groups. Hitler was also a master of body language. He knew how to get people to trust him quickly. In his speeches he promised economic recovery and a way out for Germany. Expanding propaganda and a growing party base supported his autocratic skills. He presented a beautiful vision of the future, a vision of a country that was independent of the Treaty of Versailles and independent of other states. He pledged to bring back the power of the past, to build a strong army, a strong economy, and to rebuild the cities. How could you not trust him? You could say that at a time of poverty, these declarations were the only alternative.

 *Germany was struggling with economic problems, unemployment and poverty. There was a general pessimism caused by a lower standard of living. The nation was tired and this led to demoralisation. They wanted to get rid of the problems and expected a quick solution.*

I am sure that right-wing extremism and its idea of creating a strong state would still find many supporters today. The conclusion is that it was not the German community that was evil. We will never know how many countries would have followed the same path in similar circumstances.

Nazi symbolism also played a key role in its popularity.

The cult of discipline, order and strength attracted many Germans. The Nazis created a sense of community by using simple symbols and appealing to tradition. People willingly gathered in large numbers for Hitler's speeches. This was how he gained support and new followers. Using modern media such as radio, combined with traditional media, was another way the Nazis used to shape public opinion and win political support.

Why were the Jews so hated? The answer is simple. The Jewish people were the ones who could best deal with the effects of the economic crisis. Jews in Europe (including Germany) ran all kinds of businesses, were able to adapt to the prevailing economic conditions and, above all, helped each other. Before the Nazis came to power, Jews were active in many areas of society. They were entrepreneurs, scientists, artists, lawyers, doctors and other professionals. Jews were also active in social organisations and involved in various aspects of life. If the average German had nothing to live on and the Jews managed to live well, where was the justice? The Jewish people did not have a country of their own, so there was no possibility of deporting them. Other solutions had to be found, and Hitler offered them. He believed that no other people than the German people could feel at home in countries belonging to the Aryan race. When the Nazi Party came to power it began to blame the Jews for all the evils that Germany was going through. Anti-Semitic slogans appealed to many, and Adolf Hitler, who was fluent in public speaking, cleverly adapted his arguments by manipulating public sentiment. He held the Jews responsible for losing the First World War and for the restrictions imposed on Germany by the Treaty of Versailles. The Jews, regarded as a merchant class, were accused of enriching themselves at the expense of German society. They were considered to be those who plotted against the Germans. In a society in turmoil and struggling economically, conspiracy theories gained popularity. In the years that followed, after the Nazis came to power, ordinary German citizens became involved in the persecution of Jews. During Kristallnacht, citizens attacked Jewish shops and homes. Jews were harassed and persecuted, and this was before the extermination began. By the late 1920s and early 1930s, Nazi ideology was adapted to meet social expectations and went beyond anti-Semitism.

The Night of Broken Glass (in German: Kristallnacht) - a pogrom against Jews in the Third Reich, organised by the NSDAP on the night of 9-10 November 1938. 91 Jews were murdered, 171 synagogues were burned down, 7,500 shops and businesses were looted and destroyed (the name Kristallnacht comes from broken glass), 26,000 Jews were deported to concentration camps. Kristallnacht marked the beginning of a period of increased persecution of Jews in Nazi Germany[91].

---

[91] source: Encyklopedia PWN, entry: Noc kryształowa (accessed 17/11/2023).

Now you know what the Germans were envious of in the Jews and why they put their trust in Hitler. What were the psychological arguments behind it? Is it possible to become a Nazi quickly? You probably believe that no ideology can turn you into an emotionless creature. Are you sure? And have you ever heard of the Third Wave experiment?

The need to belong is one of the basic human desires that drives us to cross the boundaries between good and evil in order to achieve it.

People are capable of making decisions that are morally wrong only when they are expected to do so by the group they belong to. The human mind has the ability to justify any action.
An ordinary person faced with a choice between 'security' and 'freedom' will always choose 'security'.

The promise of belonging to a group where the rules are respected and there is a sense of security will always be tempting. These desires motivate us to make certain decisions and life choices[92].

In the 1960s in the United States, an unconventional experiment was carried out in one of the schools. The experiment, later called the Third Wave, was conducted by Ron Jones, a history teacher at a California high school, whose students wanted to find out how it was possible that civilized German society supported the ideology of the Nazis. Jones decided to conduct a spontaneous sociological experiment to uncover the mechanisms of attracting people to specific ideas and values. This improvised experiment was intended to encourage students to actively support the initiative. He asked what makes people engage in specific ideas because he wanted to understand what makes people participate in specific projects. The experiment aimed to discover the motivational factors that lead people to engage with ideas and to understand how these factors influence the process of forming

---

[92]   Information taken from the documentary 'Lesson Plan' by P. Neel, D. Jeffery 2010.

beliefs and loyalty in a social group.

The experiment started on Monday. In the first lesson, the teacher introduced the students to the world of discipline, presenting the characteristic elements of a totalitarian system. He stressed the importance of discipline, comparing it to the effort of an athlete, ballet dancer or painter working towards perfection. He defined discipline as the exchange of physical hardship for the development of mental skills. He emphasised its role in self-development and self-control. To make students feel the power of discipline, he told them to sit in a chair in the right way. He instructed them in posture and focused their attention on details. He found that the students quickly accepted the exercise, which inspired him to go further. He introduced new rules, such as sitting up straight, the need to always have a pencil and notebook with them, the obligation to answer questions in three words and only when asked. He also manipulated the volume of answers and rewarded effort for correct answers. Gradually, the whole group engaged with the lesson and became disciplined.

The next day, all the students sat as they were told and the teacher continued the experiment. He emphasised the value of community and belonging, recalling his experiences as an athlete, coach and historian. He introduced the following slogans: **'Strength through discipline'**, **'Strength through unity'**, **'Strength through action'** and encouraged the students to repeat them over and over again. They began to feel the power of belonging to a group through shared experiences. This strengthened their bonds. Jones also created a welcoming gesture, the **Third Wave** salute, to symbolise strength. He introduced a new policy for students to use it outside of class. They quickly adopted the new practice of greeting each other, attracting the attention of other students who wanted to join in.

On Wednesday (the third day), the teacher handed out membership cards of the Third Wave movement to the students. He marked the three selected cards with a red 'X' and told their holders that they had a special task to report to him about students who did not follow the established class rules. In other words, they were to report on others. Jones depicted the impact of discipline on society, the nature of responsibility for ones' actions and self-reliance. The individual will sacrifice everything to protect the community. He also stressed the importance of hard work and mutual loyalty to achieve new goals. Students were given specific tasks to complete. For example, they could design a Third Wave banner, prevent intruders entering the classroom, convince other children in a nearby primary school of the benefits of sitting correctly, or write down the name and address of a trusted friend who would like to join. A procedure for accepting new members was introduced. The newcomers had to prove that they knew the rules of the group and agreed to abide by them. But on that day, the teacher felt anxious. In the end, around twenty students came forward with information about offences, suggesting that half the class felt obliged to report on their peers, despite the fact that three students had been designated to report inappropriate behaviour in the classroom. The Third Wave movement affected the school's learning timetable, with students from other classes escaping to attend Ron Jones' events.

That day, Jones realised that things had gone too far and decided to slow this down. Speaking to the assembled room of over 80 people already seated in silence, he reflected on pride. His message was that pride is much more than flags and salutes. It is an intangible value. No one can take it away. Pride is the awareness of being the best, invulnerable to destruction. It is a national political movement aimed at identifying young leaders who can lead the country in the right direction. Those attending were presented as a special group of young people chosen to help achieve this. They could change the nation's destiny, giving it a new sense of community, if they learnt lessons from the experience. He said that the following day, Friday at noon, a presidential candidate (invented by Ron) would announce the official formation of a youth organisation called the Third Wave. At the same time, more than a thousand youth organisations from across the country would show their resounding support for the movement. As the press would be present at the event, the students were asked if they were ready to look nice and represent the school proudly. There was no laughter, or resistance. They were excited about the upcoming event and whispered about what they would wear and who they would invite.

By the fifth day (Friday), before noon, the room was filled with more than 200 students, and the Third Wave posters covered every free space on the walls. Jones had set up a screen in the middle of the room to broadcast the presidential candidate's speech. There were also fictional journalists pretending to be friends of the teacher. The students sat in perfect attention, staring at the screen. The school hall turned into a place filled with excitement, as if something very special was about to happen.

Jones, standing in the centre, gestured to salute and the 200 attendees immediately responded by doing the same. 'Strength through discipline,' he said, and the students responded again. He asked them to do what he wanted and explained how important the event was. Everyone trembled and then a loud cry of 'Strength through discipline!' broke out. The teacher switched on the screen, but for a long time only a blue background was visible. Ten minutes later while everyone kept staring at the screen, one of the students broke the silence and by shouting, 'There is no leader, is there'? Everyone's eyes turned to the student, then back to the screen. The teacher stood in front of it: 'There is no leader! There is no Third Wave movement. You thought you were the chosen ones, better than the others. Now, we could all empathise with Nazi Germany and see how society is manipulated'.

Jones then showed photos from the Nazi party congress and displayed statements by the soldiers justifying their brutality towards others, such as: 'I was just doing my duty', 'I was just following orders'.

What are the conclusions here? In a few days an ambitious

American teacher created a nucleus of young Nazis. He turned young people, who had grown up in a world of freedom, into a community dedicated to discipline and ideas. Moreover he did it without attacking or hating anyone.

Concepts such as 'discipline' and 'collaboration' are associated with values that give meaning to human life.

The student movement fulfilled basic human needs such as the maintenance of social order, a sense of belonging and being valued. It set challenging goals and gave a sense of being better than others. Ron Jones became a role model for the students as a true leader. Because there was no criticism of the Third Wave activities, the students trusted him easily. Throughout the experiment, only a few (three sceptical students) tried to disrupt the teacher's leadership[93].

Jones was surprised by the results of the experiment.

In a very short time, the innocent teenagers became supporters of nationalism. The experiment showed the human tendency to be easily manipulated, especially at a young age. Young people want to be part of an elite community, do not want to stand out from the crowd and do not want to be bullied. They want to fit in and avoid being made fun of. They are more vulnerable to outside influences. In 1967, young people created the Third Wave. This was the case in Germany just thirty years ago.

> **HITLERJUGEND - NSDAP** youth organisation, active from 1926 to 1945; educated youth in racism, chauvinism and militarism. From 1936 it was the only youth organisation in the Third Reich. During the Second World War, members of the organisation performed military auxiliary service.

---

[93] Information taken from the documentary 'Lesson Plan' by P. Neel, D. Jeffery 2010.

Fascism, according to Ron Jones - the man behind the Third Wave experiment[94]:
- complete trust in one leader,
- positive self-perception as part of the group,
- complete trust in the group as a guide for one's life,
- protection of all values and truths proclaimed by the group,
- harming those who attack the ideology,
- a sense of superiority over people outside the group,
- abuse of power.

Now you know how easily you can be indoctrinated. Stay alert! Have you ever heard of such techniques of controling people's minds? And have you ever heard about them in school?

 *Why do we learn in school what does not seem interesting and will not be useful to us in our future lives, and why do we not learn about the mechanisms of manipulation?*

I want you to think about it. Develop your social awareness and resistance to manipulation outside of school. What can protect you from manipulation is knowledge of human emotions and the motives behind people's actions. Psychology is a science that helps to understand the mechanisms of human relationships and to improve communication. Such an experiment should certainly be an important voice in the global debate on education.

There are also other studies whose authors have tried to discover the motives behind the behaviour of the German people during the Nazi dictatorship, and to investigate how far people are capable of going when ordered to cross the boundaries of morality. In 1962, Stanley Milgram conducted an experiment in which participants administered electric shocks

---

[94] https://pafere.org/2021/11/10/artykuly/sprawdz-czy-przypadkiem-nie-jestes-faszysta (accessed 22/11/2023).

at the command of another person[95]. Another experiment was a prison experiment carried out at Stanford University. Students played the roles of prisoners and the guards who tormented them[96]. The results of these experiments confirmed the popular thesis of 'the banality of evil'. According to this theory, people in dictatorships tend to mindlessly follow orders and commit atrocities. This is because their ethical principles are suppressed by the will of others and dissolve in collective action. Collective terror results in the human need to conform and to be obeyed.

It means that the desire to be seen as 'normal' is stronger than the desire to be compassionate to those around us. It might suggest that someone committing atrocities is not fully responsible for their actions. Those who are surrounded by violence begin to see it as normalised and accepted.

Let me share another experiment by the psychologist Albert Bandura, author of social learning theory. Two groups of children were given a doll named Bobo to play with. The children in one group watched adults play with the doll and imitated them, while the children in the other group watched adults use violence against the doll and then did the same[97]. In other words, people absorb the methods of violence and literally learn them.

Let's go back to Nazi Germany and the public schools. To conclude German educational system, here are two mathematics assignments from a German state school in the 1930s[98]:

---

[95] https://dobrebadania.pl/eksperyment-milgrama-ang-milgram-experiment (accessed 22/11/2023).

[96] https://dobrebadania.pl/stanfordzki-eksperyment-wiezienny-ang-stanford-prison-experiment/ (accessed 22/11/2023).

[97] A. Bandura, *Teoria społecznego uczenia się*, Warszawa 2010. pp. 49-50.

[98] http://old.uwazamrze.pl/artykul/1008252/szkoly-masowego-razenia/3 (accessed 22/11/2023).

1. It costs about four marks a day to look after a mentally ill person. There are currently 300,000 mentally ill people in state care. How much does it cost to look after them? How many honeymoon loans of 1,000 marks could be granted with this money?

2. A plane takes off to attack the international Jewish centre in Warsaw. It bombs the city. When it took off with a full load of bombs and 100 kg of fuel in the tank, the plane weighed about 8 tonnes. On its return, the remaining load weighed 230 kg. The aeroplane takes off with 12 dozen bombs, each weighing 10 kg. What is the weight of the empty aeroplane?

Doesn't this sound ridiculous?

Let's move on to the next chapter of the book...

Chapter II

Medical experiments
on prisoners
in German camps

In this chapter, I will take you behind the scenes of Nazi politics. Here, medicine became a tool of destruction and human life was treated as an experimental material. This part of the book will take us deep into the dark past, where human dignity was not respected. We will discover the human capacity for cruelty, where ordinary people were the victims of inhuman treatment and the cruellest forms of torture.

Experiment means an attempt, a scientific experience. An experiment is 'the deliberate induction of a particular phenomenon (or a change in it) under laboratory conditions in order to study and explain its course'[99]. Nowadays, a medical experiment is a study carried out on a human being in order to obtain a direct benefit for the health of a particular patient or, in a broader sense, for many patients. Such research can be conducted under appropriate sterile conditions and under the supervision of the best doctors. Doctors use new methods when the current ones are not effective. In this chapter I would like to argue that the medical experiments carried out in the German camps should not be considered in 'medical' categories. The methods used by the doctors of the Third Reich should be called 'pseudo-medical experiments'.

After the end of the war, the trial of Nazi doctors at the US Military Tribunal revealed experiments on prisoners in German concentration camps. Some 350 doctors were involved, according to sources[100]. This was based on Hitler's idea that enemies of the

---

[99] Collective work, Encyklopedia Popularna PWN, entry: Eksperyment, Warszawa 2020.
[100] J. Mikulski, *Medycyna hitlerowska w służbie III Rzeszy*, Warszawa 1981, p. 9.

state would benefit the Reich by working or dying. A variety of criteria, such as racial, political or professional, were used to select SS doctors. It mattered whether a physician joined the SS before or after graduating in medicine. The medics who were sent to work in the concentration camps were fully committed to the Nazi ideology and convinced of the need to put it into practice. The medical oath, Primum non nocere (first, do no harm), had no meaning for the doctors of the Third Reich.

Before the end of the Second World War, medical experiments were performed in various camps, including Buchenwald, Auschwitz-Birkenau, Ravensbrück, Dachau, Mathausen-Gusen, Natzweiler-Struthof, Neuengamme and Sachsenhausen[101]. As a rule, operations required the approval of the SS leadership. However, the SS health service was responsible for their organisation. Nevertheless, there were unplanned experiments carried out on the initiative of the camp doctors themselves, often without the knowledge of the leadership. Experiments were also carried out in the camps: Mittelbau-Dora, Gross-Rosen, Stutthof, Majdanek and Flossenbürg[102].

There were five categories of experiments[103]:
- *infectious diseases,*
- *racial experiments,*
- *war medicine,*
- *therapeutic experiments,*
- *other medical experiments.*

Prisoners selected for experiments were usually taken to hospitals by force. It was rare for prisoners to consent to procedures on their own bodies. On Himmler's orders, experiments were mainly carried out on foreigners sentenced to death.

---

[101] S. Sterkowicz, *Zbrodnicze eksperymenty medyczne w obozach koncentracyjnych Trzeciej Rzeszy*, Warszawa 1981, p. 7.

[102] D. Jarosiński, *Eksperymenty medyczne na ludziach w niemieckich nazistowskich obozach koncentracyjnych*, [in:] Studenckie Zeszyty Naukowe, Zeszyt 17, Lublin 2008, p. 21.

[103] J. Mikulski, *Medycyna hitlerowska…*, op. cit., p. 92.

The victims of the experiments were Poles, Russians, Jews and Gypsies, regardless of their sentence. In October 1942, Himmler issued an order commuting the sentences of Gestapo prisoners to life imprisonment in the camp on condition that the victims survived the experiments. Poles and Russians were excluded. They would die regardless of the results[104].

Concentration camps were part of the 'final solution' policy. But they were also a place where less experienced surgeons could gain experience before starting their professional careers. Prisoners were treated as excellent research material. Research became a career ladder for many German doctors. The medical staff did what they could to minimise the side effects of the experiments[105].

People who were ill or undergoing experiments were accommodated in the hospital. It was divided into smaller units according to the type of illness. Sanitary and living conditions were similar in all units. Five or six people usually slept in a single bed made of paper mattresses woven together. There were no medicines in the camps and patients were given small rations of food. In most cases the patients suffered from digestive problems, mainly diarrhoea, and due to lack of strength they often met their physiological needs in bed. The hospital was filled with moaning, screaming and the sounds of suffering. There was a shortage of medical staff and the ward was a place of natural selection, with many patients dying of starvation or getting infected[106].

The doctors working in the concentration camps were mainly responsible for selecting prisoners, signing death certificates and supervising punishments and executions. Much of the medical staff was made up of young people who hadn't yet finished studying and who didn't have any qualifications. They tried and tested their skills in the camps and took no responsibility for the decisions they made.

---

[104] T. Musioł, *Dachau 1933 – 1945*, Katowice 1968, p. 197.

[105] M. Jankowski, 'Zbrodnicza medycyna w obozach koncentracyjnych III Rzeszy' [in:] Papricana. Humanities journal, 18/10/2012.

[106] E. Klee, *Auschwitz medycyna III Rzeszy i jej ofiary*, Kraków 2005, pp. 22-23.

On 28 February 1931, the circular letter was signed by the Minister of the Interior of the German Reich setting out rules for medical treatment, research methods and scientific experiments on human race. Despite the seemingly humane nature of the document, there was little respect for the rules by doctors or the Nazi authorities. Experiments could be officially conducted under the following conditions[107]:

- legitimate reasons for a positive outcome,
- reduction of pain,
- elimination of life-threatening risks,
- adherence to ethical medical principles and standards during procedures.

The regulations also required the patient's consent to the study, but this could be revoked at any time. Under the document, experiments could not be carried out on children and adolescents under the age of 18 or on people who were dying. In the concentration camps, however, the reality was quite different. Prisoners were treated as an inferior population, as subhuman. The circular letter was used during the trial against the criminal doctors at the American Military Tribunal in Nuremberg[108].

On 28 July 1942, Adolf Hitler issued a decree on sanitary services and health care. Following this, Karl Brandt became General Commissioner for Health and Sanitation. He was tasked with solving the problems of the military and civilian health services, but his efforts were unsuccessful. In 1943 Brandt was promoted to head of medical supplies and coordinator of medical research, and in August 1944 he became Reich Commissioner for Health and Sanitation, one of the highest positions in the Reich government structure[109].

---

[107] U. Völklein, *Josef Mengele. Doktor z Auschwitz*, Warszawa 2011, p. 12.

[108] S. Sterkowicz, *Zbrodnicze eksperymenty medyczne...*, op. cit., p. 280.

[109] H. J. Neumann, *Czy Hitler był chory?*, Warszawa 2011, p. 111.

Heinrich Himmler had a huge influence over the experiments on prisoners of war in the camp, issuing detailed guidelines to the doctors. The doctors were obliged to inform him of all research and its results. Himmler's involvement in, and support for, experimentation is confirmed by numerous documents he sent to scientists. He commissioned research on human endurance at low temperatures and on pressure changes. He also received letters from Dr Ernst Grawitz with the results of experiments on the poisonous chemical substance 'N-Stoff'[110].

The German Ancestral Heritage Association, headed by Himmler himself, played an important role in the medical experiments[111]. After the Association was incorporated into Himmler's staff, the Research Institute for Defence Purposes was established, with research facilities in the camps, including Natzweiler-Struthof camp and Dachau camp. In August 1943, chief SS doctors were appointed in each district, supervised by a senior SS and police commander. The criminal police also assisted in the selection of prisoners for medical experiments. The SS garrison doctor performed administrative functions and supervised the SS crew. In the larger camps there was also a group of SS doctors in the military units (SS-truppenärzte), and prisoners were supervised by camp doctors (SS-lagerärzte), dentists (SS-zahnärzte) and pharmacists (SS-lagerapothekern)[112].

Organisational changes in 1942 gave the camp medical service independence, with the garrison doctor reporting to the concentration camp medical head. Contrary to their stated duties, the camp doctors focused on selecting prisoners for extermination, neglecting medical care. The planning of medical experiments was a matter for Himmler's approval, and was both his and others' initiative. Individual doctors were responsible for specific studies. Many experiments were initiated by the camp doctors themselves. In fact, the intensity

---

[110] D. Jarosiński, *Eksperymenty medyczne…*, op. cit., p. 23.

[111] http://majdanek.com.pl/eksperymenty/eksperymenty.html (accessed 24/11/2023).

[112] Ibidem.

of the experiments reached its peak in 1942. Prisoners were deliberately infected with infectious diseases: **malaria, typhus, tuberculosis, gas gangrene, viral hepatitis** and **septicaemia**. Camp doctors also studied how the human body reacted to extreme conditions, such as **high** and **low body temperatures. Children** were also experimented on in the search for effective methods of mass sterilisation. The camps became a place for research into **nutrition, body detoxification** and **surgical operations** on both sick and healthy prisoners, with the aim of improving the skills of doctors. **Biological weapons** and **toxic munitions** were also tested. Much of this research was carried out on behalf of pharmaceutical and chemical companies[113].

Below are selected experiments from six concentration camps.

Auschwitz-Birkenau Concentration Camp

First, some basic information about the camp. Auschwitz, the German Nazi concentration and extermination camp, is the most universally recognised symbol of the Holocaust, the site of mass genocide. No other camp or extermination centre was used to exterminate the Jewish people, representing almost all of occupied Europe, on such a large scale. It should be noted that up to 40% of the registered prisoners at Auschwitz were Poles. Roma, Soviet prisoners of war and people of more than twenty different nationalities also suffered and died in the camp. The Auschwitz Concentration Camp was established in 1940 and, from 1942, functioned primarily as a place for the extermination of Jews. The history of the camp falls into two periods[114]:

- from 1940 to mid-1942, the majority of deportees and victims were Poles. Established 10 months after the outbreak of war, Auschwitz was one of the main sites for the deportation and extermination of Poles,

---

[113] J. Wieliczka-Szarek, *III Rzesza. Narodziny i zmierzch szaleństwa*, Kraków 2006, p. 98.

[114] https://auschwitz.org/ (accessed 26/11/2023).

- from mid-1942 to 1944, the majority of deportees and victims were Jews. Auschwitz was the largest extermination centre for Jews from the territories occupied by the Third Reich. The intensity of extermination in the second phase was many times greater, with Jews making up almost 85% of the deportees and about 90% of the victims throughout the camp's existence.

In the early days there was one main camp, Auschwitz, established in June 1940. This included the central administration, the political section, the garrison management, the main supply warehouses, workshops and SS companies, where most of the camp's prisoners worked. In March 1942, a subcamp of the Auschwitz camp was established, known as Birkenau. Its name derives from the German name of the village Brzezinka where it was located. Birkenau was the site of the largest mass extermination units in Europe: gas chambers and crematoria, where Nazi torturers killed most of the Jews deported to the camp. Birkenau was also used to store and systematically kill the sick and those selected for extermination from all the camps. In October 1942 the Auschwitz-Monowitz subcamp was established. The name comes from the village of Monowitz (Polish: Monowice) where it was located. The camp provided German companies with prisoners for slave labour, which led the Nazis to set up subcamps in nearby industrial plants. In total, nearly 50 different subcamps were established between 1942 and 1945[115].

Auschwitz-Birkenau camp - three groups of medical pseudo-experiments:
- biological - research into race and all related aspects such as heredity, fertility reduction; research into typhus, early detection of cervical cancer, starvation disease; simulations of ulcers and infectious hepatitis,

---

[115] Ibidem.

- pharmacological - research into new drugs and their side effects in humans,
- surgical - related to expanding doctors' knowledge and practice of surgery[116].

Within the first group, research into maintaining the purity of the Nordic race was particularly important. There were experiments on heredity, especially with twins. The Germans saw this as an opportunity to create an ideal large population in half the time of a single birth. Dr Josef Mengele was responsible for carrying out the experiments. The research was funded by the German Research Committee headed by Prof O. von Verschuer, who was Director of the Institute of Anthropology, Human Heredity, and Eugenics[117].

Dr Mengele personally selected his victims, and usually did so as soon as they arrived at the camp. According to witnesses, some 350 pairs of twins of both sexes aged 2-16 were sent to the camp[118]. Documents in the Auschwitz Memorial archives confirm the approximate number of victims. There are 125 names with camp numbers on the handwritten list. It includes boys, adult men and twins brought to the camp between 1943 and 1944 from the Terezín ghetto and areas of what was then Hungary. There is also a record of 111 Jewish twins of both sexes who were placed in the women's camp. According to the account of one of these twins, Otto Klein, there were about 107 people aged between 4 and 60 in barrack 15 in section BIIf. Most of them were Jewish children from Hungary, the Czech Republic, Germany, Italy, Belgium and France. At the end of the experiments, most of the twins were killed so that they could be dissected and analysed for comparison. Only a few survived. Here is what former prisoner Vera Aleksander said: '(...) The next day the SS took the two boys I was looking after. One of them was hunchbacked. After two

---

[116] M. Nyiszli, *Pracownia doktora Mengele. Wspomnienia lekarza z Oświęcimia*, Warszawa 1966, p. 21.

[117] http://majdanek.com.pl/eksperymenty/auschwitz.html (accessed 21/11/2023).

[118] Memoirs of Elżbieta Warszawska, employed as a nurse in Auschwitz [in:] http://majdanek.com.pl/eksperymenty/auschwitz.html (accessed 21/11/2023).

or three days the SS man brought them back horribly injured. They had cut wounds. The boy with the hunchback had been sewn back together with his brother, their wrists had also been sewn together. You could smell the terrible stench of gangrene. The wounds were dirty and the children cried all night'[119]. The third and decisive part of the experiments followed. The internal organs were analysed. The children were usually killed by intracardiac injection of phenol or evipan, followed by a detailed autopsy. Important research material was preserved and sent to the Berlin Institute. To ensure speedy transport, the parcels were stamped: 'Urgent, important for war purposes'[120].

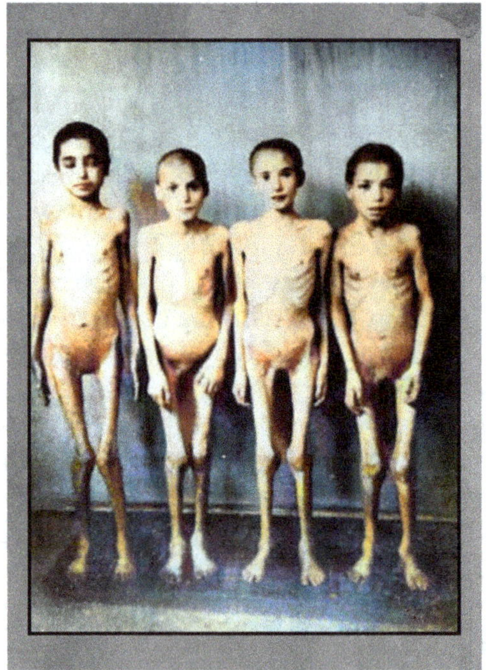

Photo 5. Twins who aroused the scientific interest of camp doctors during medical experiments in Auschwitz[121].

---

[119] Ibidem.

[120] Ibidem.

[121] Photo: public domain.

Each twin was given a detailed questionnaire covering their appearance, medical history and development. They were also photographed, x-rayed and examined regularly. The examinations were then compared with each other. Urine was tested and blood was taken and sent to the Waffen-SS Hygienic and Bacteriological Research Station in Rajsk or to the Institute for Anthropology and Eugenics in Berlin to be tested if certain protein reactions needed to be studied. The twins underwent intelligence tests, neurological examinations and other special procedures. In order to compare their reactions, they were given blood transfusions and injections of foreign substances or pathogens. To compare reactions to pain, surgical procedures were conducted without anaesthesia. Autopsies were usually carried out on both twins, so that when one twin died, the other was killed by an injection of phenol. A detailed autopsy protocol was prepared[122].

The twins were examined regularly in the camp. They were marked and stamped. Stamps were stuck on their bodies and the distance between them was measured and marked by a pencil. A ruler and compass were used for measuring. The child's height and weight were taken, as well as medical histories of past illnesses, dental impressions, fingerprints and even shoe soles. People with dwarfism were also studied by Dr Mengele[123].

Other experiments involved injecting healthy children and healthy adults with noma germs[124]. Witnesses reported a rapid deterioration of cheek tissue and a sudden increase in the number of deaths. Approximately 3,000 people, mostly children, died as a result of being injected with noma germs. Dr Mengele directed this research while trying to find effective ways to treat the Wehrmacht Soldiers. Corpses with a particularly unusual appearance were delivered to camp photographer Wilhelm

---

[122] U. Völklein, *Josef Mengele…*, op. cit., p. 155.

[123] U. Völklein, *Josef Mengele…*, op. cit., p. 155-156.

[124] Noma germs cause a disease called noma. Noma is a progressive inflammation of the face and mouth. Today, the disease affects children in communities experiencing poverty, malnutrition and poor hygiene.

Brass. 'Sometimes corpses of children who had died of noma were brought to the photo studio. On Mengele's orders, photographs were taken, but not of the whole body and not naked, but only of the upper part of the body, including the head and parts of the face with traces of the disease. He also ordered that the heads be separated from the torso and preserved in jars of formalin'[125].

Prisoners were subjected to electric shocks to see how much voltage a person could withstand before dying. This brutal procedure resulted in many deaths. Those who survived were sent to the gas chamber. Test devices were attached to the prisoners' legs, arms and temples, and the procedure took between 30 and 45 minutes. One witness reported: 'The women undergoing the tests were convulsing. Some had foam coming out of their mouths and others had tissues pushed into their mouths. After the devices were disconnected, I saw no burns on their bodies. Instead, I saw that in many cases the prisoners [...] were dead when they had to be removed'[126].

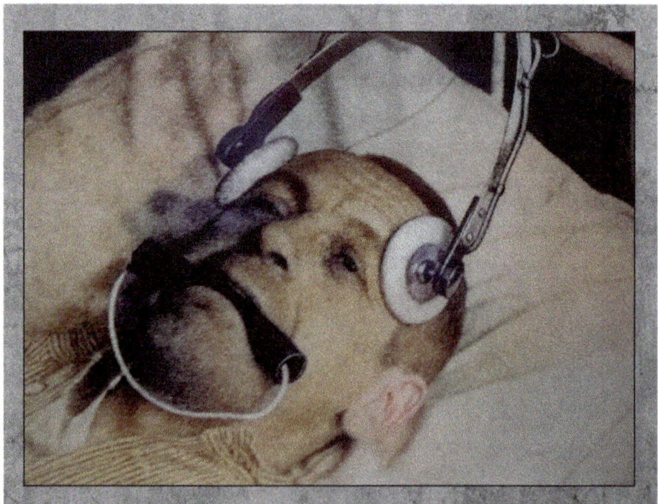

Photo 6. The photo shows an electric shock experiment carried out on a camp prisoner

---

125 U. Völklein, *Josef Mengele…*, op. cit., p. 160.
126 Ibidem, p. 280-281.

An important research project at Auschwitz was sterilisation. Dr Mengele undertook to find a method of sterilising large numbers of women in a short time, undetected. He was given the Auschwitz camp and about 800 Jewish women transferred from Ravensbrück. Mengele carried out brutal operations to castrate the women. The operations resulted in health problems and death. One of the methods used to deprive women of their fertility was the injection of acid to cause adhesions in the fallopian tubes or the use of hormones to stop menstruation. Women who survived suffered severe stomach pains and bleeding. Inflammation and paralysis occurred as a result of the contrast medium penetrating the peritoneum[127]. The experiments were carried out mainly on Gypsy and Jewish women, including young girls, and the exact number of victims is not known. Both women and men were exposed to extremely high doses of X-rays, causing painful burns to the skin. There was also surgical removal of the testicles, but Dr Mengele found this method too time-consuming. The camp also experimented on 'Spanish fly' and other aphrodisiacs to increase the libidos and fertility of war-weary German soldiers[128].

Research into the modification of the iris of the human eye was also part of the work at Auschwitz. Prisoners with atypical iris colours were selected and killed. Their eyeballs were then sent to an institute in Berlin. Dr Mengele was particularly interested in one prisoner with a different iris colour. He injected adrenaline into his eyes to change the colour, but this did not happen. This research, like the others, brought nothing but great suffering[129].

Human bodies and their parts of scientific value were sent to the Institute of Hereditary, Anthropology, and Eugenics in Berlin.

These included eyeballs, blood samples from twins, atypical human skeletons, foetuses and neonates of identical and fraternal twins, and internal organs from children and adults.

---

127 http://majdanek.com.pl/eksperymenty/auschwitz.html (accessed 21/11/2023).

128 U. Völklein, *Josef Mengele…*, op. cit., p. 163.

129 Ibidem, p.167.

They were interested in all unusual cases such as double organs in one body, etc.[130]

The Germans were keen to develop an effective typhus vaccine to protect German soldiers fighting on the Eastern Front (mainly in the Balkans), where typhus was highly concentrated. Pharmaceutical companies[131] supplied new medicines such as B-1012, B-1034, Ruthenium, Eleudron and Prontosil for testing on prisoners. These drugs had not been tested before. Sulphonamide mixtures and typhoid drugs were given as tablets, granules, liquids, injections and rectal infusions in varying doses. If the experiment was successful, they were to be introduced for general use[132].

Photo 7. Pharmaceuticals tested[133].

The selected prisoners, whether sick or intentionally infected, were forbidden to take any medication except those prescribed by the doctor. They were systematically submitted to laboratory tests and X-rays. The doctors were obliged to keep precise records

---

[130] Ibidem, p.168.

[131] I cannot name any pharmaceutical company at this point as they are still on the market today.

[132] https://lekcja.auschwitz.org/2022_medycyna_pl/ (accessed 21/11/2023).

[133] Photo: public domain.

of what they'd done. Unfortunately, the drugs did not bring the expected results, and patients complained of side effects such as nausea, digestive disorders, cyanosis, shortness of breath, bloody diarrhoea and even collapse. Post-mortems were carried out on those who died to identify any internal organ injuries[134].

Surgical operations were also carried out in the camp, both by qualified doctors and by medical students and SS non-commissioned officers who were driven by curiosity. Surgeries were intended to improve medical practice and to satisfy ambitions. Unfortunately, they were often carried out completely unnecessarily and caused additional suffering to the prisoners. They usually involved the amputation of limbs, the removal of appendages, the removal of gall bladders or the incision of abscesses. The operations were often spontaneous and uncontrolled, and the number of victims is unknown[135].

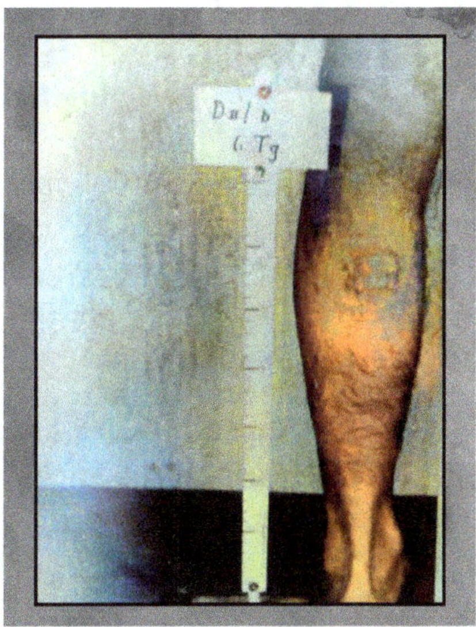

Photo 8. Effects of experiments by a Wehrmacht doctor - Auschwitz Concentration Camp[136].

---

[134] Y. Ternon, S. Helman, *Historia medycyny SS czyli mit rasizmu biologicznego*, Warszawa 1973, pp. 83-85.

[135] D. Jarosiński, *Eksperymenty…*, op. cit., p. 23.

[136] Photo: public domain.

Research into starvation diseases was also carried out in Auschwitz. They focused on changes in the internal organs as a result of malnutrition and starvation. Doctors condemned selected prisoners to death by starvation. Before they were given a heart injection of phenol, they were questioned about their medical history. They were asked about their weight, what medicines they were taking and photographed. Post-mortems were carried out and histopathological samples taken from the liver, pancreas and spleen[137]. There was also research into cervical cancer in the camp. Female prisoners were examined with a colposcope[138]. If lesions in the reproductive organs were suspected, women were subjected to further treatment, including the taking of histopathological sections, which were sent to an institute in Berlin for analysis. In all, about 50 female prisoners underwent such a procedure[139].

The doctors in Auschwitz violated professional ethics by overstepping what they considered to be the boundaries of morality. They created their own space, free from the law. They disregarded the promises of the Book of Hippocrates, a set of ethical principles for physicians to which they committed themselves in their professional practice.

The oath required loyalty to the patient, medical confidentiality, responsibility and safety. In those days, performing risky medical experiments and causing death were punishable offences. Nevertheless, SS doctors were not afraid of sanctions because of their 'superiority'.

The Red Army finally entered Auschwitz on 27 January 1945. About 7,000 prisoners were released in Auschwitz I, Auschwitz II-Birkenau and Auschwitz III-Monowitz. About 500 more were

---

[137] http://majdanek.com.pl/eksperymenty/auschwitz.html (accessed 21/11/2023).

[138] Colposcope - a device used to accurately determine the condition of a woman's internal organs and to detect any changes in the cervix at an early stage.

[139] http://majdanek.com.pl/eksperymenty/auschwitz.html (accessed 21/11/2023).

set free before the Soviet army entered the camp[140]. This was the end of the largest German concentration camp in Poland.

Buchenwald Concentration Camp

Buchenwald Concentration Camp was one of the largest concentration camps in the German Reich during the Nazi era. It was built before the outbreak of the Second World War - before Germany's expansion eastwards - in July 1937 on the wooded slopes of the Ettersberg, eight kilometres north of Weimar in Thuringia. The main camp was divided into a large camp for long-term prisoners and a small camp for temporary prisoners. There was also a tent camp for political prisoners. About 130 subcamps were subordinated to Buchenwald and some of them were located far from the main camp. The largest of these was Mittelbau-Dora, near Nordhausen[141].

While only 2,561 prisoners were registered at Buchenwald when the camp opened in 1937, by February 1945 there were more than 86,000, due to the evacuation of concentration camps in Eastern Europe and the relocation of prisoners to the West. In total, some 250,000 people were imprisoned in the camp and subcamps. Initially, the camp held mainly political prisoners who opposed the Nazi ideology; later, Jews were also sent there. In all, more than 60,000 people died there, mainly as a result of inhumane working conditions, medical experiments or executions. Soviet prisoners of war were systematically executed there[142].

Most of the inmates were forced to work in the arms industry (arms factories were built near the camp). They also worked in horticulture, in the stables and in the quarry. The lucky ones got jobs in the camp administration, in the kitchen or in similar facilities. In this way they survived. The prisoners were finally

---

[140] https://auschwitz.org/media/podstawowe-informacje-o-auschwitz/ (accessed 20/11/2023).

[141] http://gelsenzentrum.de/kz_buchenwald.htm#KZ (accessed 18/11/2023).

[142] https:/weimar-lese.de/streifzuege/geschichtliches/konzentrationslager-buchenwald/ (accessed 17/11/2023).

freed by American forces on 11 April 1945[143].

The medical experiments carried out at Buchenwald mainly concerned the testing of new vaccines and drugs supplied by a large German pharmaceutical company[144] and medical institutes. The first reports of experiments date back to 15 November 1939, when a vaccine company collaborated with the camp authorities to supply diphtheria vaccines. Prisoners were also given dysentery vaccines. Due to the poor response, efforts were made to improve them. The number of prisoners used in the experiments is unknown, as are the results[145].

Between January and May 1943, prisoners were tested for the yellow fever vaccine. A total of 435 prisoners took part in the tests, which did not involve intentional infection with the disease, but only testing the body's reaction to the drug. The prisoners remained in their blocks during the experiment and were called in for follow-up results[146].

Large-scale experiments were also carried out with vaccines against typhus. Prisoners were infected in the following way: they sat on a chair with their limbs tied to it, and cages of infected insects (usually lice) were attached to their bodies. This method proved ineffective and was replaced by injections of fresh blood from typhoid patients. By the end of 1944, 24 series of experiments had been carried out on varying numbers of people, usually 40 to 60 people per series. The typhoid vaccine had a variety of origins. It was made from cultures of the yolk sac of a chicken egg, the intestines of lice, rabbit lungs, dog lungs or mouse liver. In total, about 1,000 prisoners were subjected to the experiments. The subjects were treated as follows: three groups of people were formed, all of whom were infected with typhoid fever. The first group received no treatment, the second group received a vaccine. The third group was considered a 'transitional' group, meaning

---

[143] http://gelsenzentrum.de/kz_buchenwald.htm#KZ (accessed 18/11/2023).

[144] I cannot name the pharmaceutical company at this point as it is still on the market today.

[145] http://majdanek.com.pl/eksperymenty/buchenwald.html (accessed 16/11/2023).

[146] Ibidem.

that they were injected with typhoid bacteria so that they could take part in further studies with fresh blood. The bacteria were injected directly into the muscle, intravenously or under the skin using an implant. Almost all of the volunteers in groups one and two died. Despite being vaccinated, the remaining survivors suffered serious health problems, permanent heart failure, memory loss or paralysis. The typhoid experiments had no or very little scientific value[147].

Photos 9, 10. Rooms in the camp hospital where experiments took place - Auschwitz Concentration Camp (above)[148] and Buchenwald Concentration Camp (below)[149].

---

[147] http://judentum-projekt.de/geschichte/nsverfolgung/endloesung/exp.html (accessed 17/11/2023).

[148] A private photo taken at the Auschwitz-Birkenau Memorial and Museum.

[149] Photo: public domain.

On 9 January 1943, the Plague Typhus Experimental Unit at Buchenwald was renamed the Plague Typhus and Virus Research Unit of the Waffen-SS Hygiene Institute. A week later, the Chemical-Pharmaceutical Department in Höchst began experimenting with drugs to treat typhus. The first preparations tested were called 'methyl blue' and 'acridine', which had bactericidal properties. The prisoners tested had difficulty tolerating both substances and vomited frequently - up to 12 times a day. There were also side effects such as rashes and bleeding[150].

Experiments were also carried out at Buchenwald to investigate the effects of expired blood on the human body (currently blood can be stored for up to 35 days after the addition of a preservative). Prisoners had their blood drawn and new blood introduced at the same time. The patients suffered medical difficulties, including high fever. These experiments were carried out on 92 people, but the number of deaths is unknown. It confirmed that expired blood can be harmful[151].

The camp was also involved in research into the treatment of pulmonary tuberculosis by inhaling a colloidal carbon solution. The carbon particles were supposed to stop the progression of the disease, absorb toxins and boost the body's immunity. The trials involved 45 prisoners at different stages of the disease, ten of whom were the control group. The inhalations were administered daily, and blood tests, chest X-rays, blood pressure and weight measurements were taken every 10 days. Patients were followed for two months after the experiment. There were 5 deaths in this experiment. It is not known whether the deaths were due to the experiments or to the natural course of the disease[152].

In November 1943, medicines for phosphorus burns were tested in the camp. The 'R17' was applied to fresh wounds. Two types of ointment were also being tested - echinacin and echinacin extra. Five prisoners were deliberately burned with

---

[150] http://majdanek.com.pl/eksperymenty/buchenwald.html (accessed 20/11/2023).
[151] Ibidem.
[152] Ibidem.

phosphorus from an English bomb found near Leipzig for this research. The results of this experiment are not known[153].

From the autumn of 1944, blood was taken from extremely weakened men. They were called to the laboratory after their work in the quarries. They had to do additional physical exercises until they were extremely exhausted, after which their blood was taken. The results of the tests are unknown[154].

Homosexuals were also experimented on. The experiment consisted of implanting 'artificial hormone glands' in order to 'cure' them of homosexuality. The camp doctor operated on 17 men aged between 23 and 60. The first series of operations took place on 16 September 1944, the second on 8 December. The purpose of the experiments was to determine the 'maintenance dose' and to test the effectiveness of the drug. Volunteers were given a local anaesthetic and an 'artificial gland' was implanted under the skin of their abdomen to release testosterone. They were then measured to see if their sexual inclinations changed as expected. The homosexuals were promised release if the research was successful. The promise was never kept. Within a short time, the doctor reported that the therapy was showing positive results. According to the prisoners, the treatment had changed their orientation to heterosexual, and the hormone had awakened sex drive in those who had previously been castrated.bHowever, it is suspected that the prisoners may have falsified the results. It was assumed that the treatment would not bring the intended results, especially for homosexuals[155].

Dachau Concentration Camp

Dachau Concentration Camp in Bavaria was the first of its kind. The first Nazi concentration camp in Germany was

---

[153] Ibidem.

[154] Ibidem.

[155] https://2mecs.de/wp/2008/08/buchenwald-vaernet-experimente-homosexuelle/ (accessed 22/11/2023).

established on 22 March 1933 by a decision of Heinrich Himmler, who declared: 'The camp can hold 5,000 people. Communist activists and, if necessary, marxist leaders of the Reichsbanner organisation who threaten the security of the state will be interned there if the state is overwhelmed and fails to imprison communist activists. (...) We shall take these steps, ruthlessly, in the conviction that we are acting to pacify the nation and in accordance with its feelings'[156]. This camp was the first of its kind in Germany and served as a training camp for SS men who later held the highest positions in all concentration camps. The camp was deliberately built in a swampy area with a humid and mountainous climate. It was particularly oppressive in autumn and winter, when the prisoners stood in the square for hours during roll call[157].

The camp was initially used as a propaganda tool. There were pictures taken of prisoners lined up in military formation to show the discipline of the camp. This was intended to convince the public that the camps were designed to rehabilitate. By suggesting that the camps were set up for the benefit of German citizens and that prisoners who left the camps were fully rehabilitated, the Nazis carefully manipulated public opinion. In this propaganda information machine, facts about torture and murder were deliberately omitted. In order to conceal the atrocities, committed against the prisoners, attention was drawn to the apparent positive aspects[158].

Initially, political opponents of the Nazi regime were sent to Dachau Concentration Camp. These included communists, Jews, homosexuals, Jehovah's Witnesses and criminals. After 1939, the camp filled up with prisoners from countries conquered by the Third Reich. It also became a place of extermination for

---

[156] B. Behning, *Z badań nad strukturą grup w obozie koncentracyjnym Dachau 1933-1938*, Opole 1988, p. 19.

[157] https://truthaboutcamps.eu/th/zaczelo-sie-w-rzeszy/15472,Zaczelo-sie-w-III-Rzeszy-Obozy-koncentracyjne-na-terenie-Niemiec-1933-1945.html (accessed 01/12/2023).

[158] K. Hoffmann-Curtis, *Memorials for the Dachau Concentration Camp*, 'Oxford Art Journal', 1998, vol.21(2), p. 25.

clergymen, especially Polish clergymen, who were treated with particular cruelty. Of the approximately 250,000 prisoners sent to the camp between 1933 and 1945, almost 40,000 were Polish priests, of whom about 10,000 lost their lives. The total number of prisoners is estimated at 200,000, of whom 41,500 died. The camp operated until its liberation on 29 April 1945[159].

Dachau was a place where medical experiments were carried out on a massive scale. Few prisoners consented to have their bodies examined, probably in the hope of better treatment. Priority for experiments was given to those sentenced to death, especially foreigners, mainly Poles, Russians, Jews and Gypsies[160].

Experiments in Dachau[161]:
- malaria research,
- research into the effects of low pressure on the human body,
- research into the effects of low temperature on the human body,
- experiments with sea water,
- experiments on pyoderma,
- experiments on the liver,
- research on tuberculosis,
- research on typhoid fever,
- research on blood crystallisation,
- research on blood clotting,
- surgical experiments.

The most common site for experimental research in the camp was the malaria ward. The aim of these studies was to develop a prophylactic agent that would make the human body immune to the malaria parasite. They were carried out between March 1942 and 5 April 1945, and more than 2,000 people were deliberately infected with malaria. The prisoners selected were initially young and healthy, but later included the elderly, sick

---

[159] https://truthaboutcamps.eu/th/zaczelo-sie-w-rzeszy/15472,Zaczelo-sie-w-III-Rzeszy-Obozy-koncentracyjne-na-terenie-Niemiec-1933-1945.html (accessed 01/12/2023).

[160] T. Musioł, *Dachau...*, op. cit., p. 196.

[161] Ibidem, p. 197.

and emaciated[162]. According to the regulations, everyone who arrived at the malaria station had to undergo a compulsory examination. But it was only a formal procedure. In some cases, prisoners were x-rayed. Those with large visible spots on both lungs were also included in the experiment. Many people were taken from the camps and infirmaries, brought to the station and infected with malaria. This was done in a variety of ways, most commonly by mosquito bites applied to the arm or thigh in a gas cage. Less commonly, sporozoites from the salivary glands of infected mosquitoes were injected or malaria blood was given intravenously. Occasionally, a combination infection with a mixture of malaria parasites was used, which was injected intravenously together with blood. The trial started after 10 days of infection. The patients' blood was taken every morning. The blood was then stained and examined under a microscope for malaria parasites. The doctor in charge of the study, Dr Schilling, knew more than 200 ways to treat malaria. However, he mainly used quinine, either injected intravenously or given in tablet form. The mortality rate at the malaria station itself was low. However, nearly 40 patients died as a result of exposure to malaria on other wards, and around 400 died later as a result of general exhaustion and being struck by the disease[163].

The inmates were also experimented with in high and low pressure. The experiments were related to von Braun's interplanetary space rocket research at Dora. The rockets formed the basis for the design of the V-1 and V-2 weapons. It consisted of a hermetically sealed cabin on a trolley connected to an engine and an air pump. The cabin was equipped with devices for thickening and diluting the air and had a window for observation. Between 5 and 15 prisoners were locked in the cabin to see how the human body reacted to low and high pressure. The air was then slowly or suddenly thinned and thickened,

---

[162] J. Mikulski, *Medycyna hitlerowska…*, op. cit., p. 155.
[163] T. Musioł, *Dachau…*, op. cit., pp. 198-201.

gradually reducing or increasing the atmospheric pressure[164].

Prisoners suffered the tests in different ways, depending on the atmospheric pressure set. When the pressure was lowered, they went into a frenzy - tearing their hair from their heads, cutting their faces with their fingernails, banging their heads against the wall, howling until they lost consciousness. And when the pressure was increased, the prisoners were semi-conscious. They would remain in a daze for a while until they finally dozed off. In some cases, they died as a result of a blood clot in the lungs. Autopsies revealed torn lungs, ruptured arteries, brain damage and heart failure. Parts of the brain, neck, lungs, liver, heart muscle, kidneys and limb muscles were taken from the corpses. All organs were placed in sealed containers with preservative solution and sent to the Institute of Pathology in Munich for further examination.

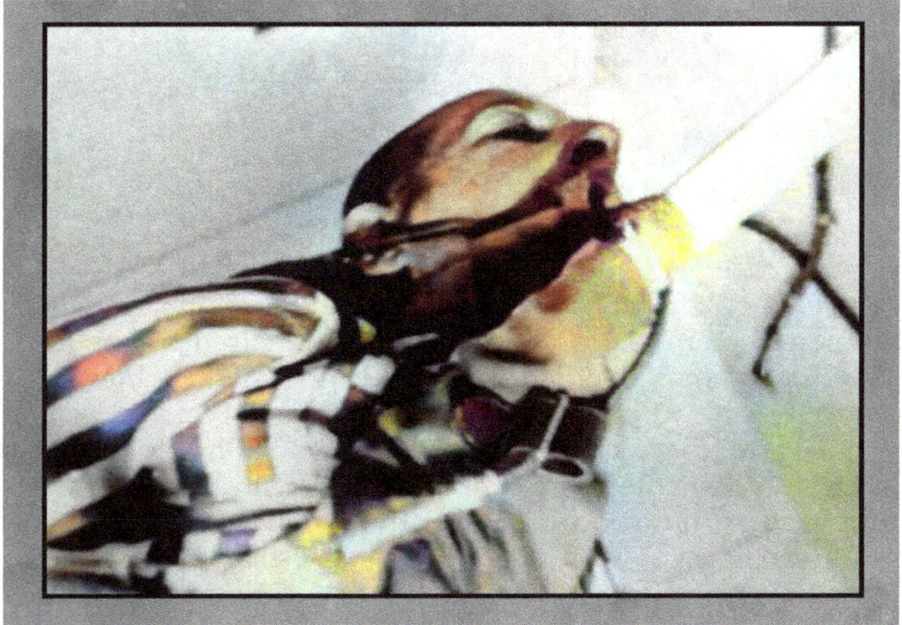

---

[164] Ibidem.

Photo 11,12: Experiment on human endurance to low and high pressure[165].

About 80 of the 320 prisoners died as a result of the low-pressure experiments. These figures do not include those who died later as a result of exhaustion caused by the tests. The experiments resulted in mental illness and widespread paralysis due to stroke[166]. The study proved that a person would not lose vital functions up to an altitude of 8,000 metres, even if they lost consciousness. Fainting occurs due to a gradual build-up of gas in the blood vessels, which is a reversible process. It has also been observed that a rapid transition from low atmospheric pressure to conditions that

---

[165] Photo: public domain.

[166] http://majdanek.com.pl/eksperymenty/dachau.html (accessed 25/11/2023).

allow breathing without the use of an oxygen apparatus does not cause significant damage to the body.

The effects of low temperatures on the human body were also the subject of research at the camp. The aim was to find ways of restoring warmth and resuscitating airmen who had crashed and frozen to death at sea. Attempts were also made to design suitable clothing for flying. The research began on 15 August 1942. In the first stage, prisoners were 'frozen' in a pool and various methods were used, including freezing in the open air. In the first stage 50-60 prisoners were allowed to take part in the experiments, in the second stage 220-240. Young, newly arrived prisoners, mostly Poles, Russians and Jews, were selected for the experiments. A few weeks before the experiments began, they were given good food and were even allowed to drink alcohol and smoke. One day they were immersed in a pool of water, naked or wearing flight suits, with or without anaesthetic. The water was cooled to 2.5 - 12 degrees until the body temperature reached about 26 degrees. Pieces of ice were thrown into the water from time to time to maintain the low temperature. After a few tens of minutes, the prisoner would lose consciousness. A lifebelt prevented him from sinking. A cable thermometer was placed in the subject's rectum to measure body temperature. Special devices recorded the reactions of the heart and other organs. A medical service monitored the submerged prisoner. At systematic intervals, the subject's blood was taken for analysis and body temperature was recorded. The duration of the experiment varied. Depending on the conditions, such a person sometimes showed vital reactions for 36 hours or more[167].

---

[167] T. Musioł, *Dachau...*, op. cit., pp. 203-204.

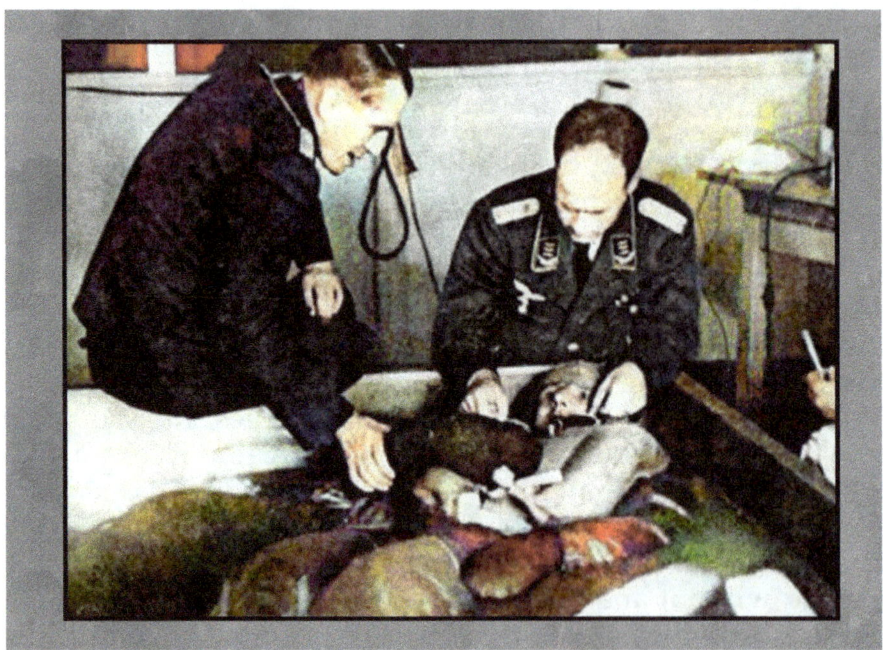

Photo 13,14: Experiment on the effects of low temperature on man[168].

---

[168] Photo: public domain.

Other prisoners, mostly Soviets, were exposed to outdoor experiments in order to check how low temperature affect people. They were left naked on stretchers outside the camp and kept in the freezing cold overnight until 9am, with cold water poured over them every hour while their body temperature was systematically measured. Most of the prisoners died as a result of these experiments. These were the most gruesome experiments carried out in Dachau. The victims moaned and screamed from the cold[169].

The lives of those exposed to low temperatures could be saved by rapid warming. Different methods were used for this: warming the prisoner in the sun, with a Sollux lamp, diathermy, hot water or massage. Himmler developed the method of heating the body with 'animal heat'. Women prisoners from the Ravensbrück camp were used for this procedure. It soon became clear, however, that the method of warming the body was not very effective, and only a few, whose physical condition allowed sexual activity, returned to normal body temperature[170].

Another type of research involved experiments with seawater to test its drinkability. The experiments began in the summer of 1944 with 44 Gypsy prisoners who had been thoroughly examined and screened. They were fed well for the first three days. Then they were starved for a week. Each had to drink half a litre of seawater a day. They were divided into five groups. Two groups were given pure seawater, and two other groups were given seawater with a salt treatment. The last group was given distilled seawater with no additives. Every day, blood, urine, faeces and saliva were collected for analysis. Most of the Gypsies endured these treatments very badly. Some would be motionless and apathetic with their eyes half closed. When they awoke, they asked for water. Their general condition was poor. They would be aggressive towards the nurses, and some would vomit. They drank dirty water from the nurses' buckets or from

---

[169]   Ibidem.

[170]   http://majdanek.com.pl/eksperymenty/dachau.html (accessed 25/11/2023).

the fire buckets, or licked water from the floor that had been spilled during washing. They lost a kilo a day. Experiments with seawater did not bring the expected results or casualties[171].

The Nazis at Dachau camp also experimented with amputating limbs and veins from healthy prisoners and transplanting them to other victims. The idea was presumably to test the reaction of living tissue in the same place in another organism. However, these experiments were inconclusive and horrific, and only added to the death toll[172].

It is also worth mentioning the so-called phlegmon ward. The participating prisoners were injected with liquid pus taken from the phlegmon and ulcers of sick or dead prisoners. The pus was injected under the skin, into the veins or into the muscles. The effects appeared on the second or third day. Some prisoners died as a result of the infection of the whole body, others developed purulent foci of phlegmon on the leg or arm, and in some cases the body did not react to the injection at all. Prisoners with purulent lesions were treated, but this treatment was brought suffering and usually ended in death or the amputation of an arm or leg. Various methods of treatment were used: surgical, allopathic, biochemical and homeopathic. Surgical therapy consisted of cutting out the infected area or puncturing the abscess and pus. This was followed by intravenous injections at 12 hours, intramuscular injections at 24 hours and subcutaneous injections at 48 hours. The patient then had a high fever with signs of intoxication and was delirious. Inflammation of the lymph nodes and veins followed the intramuscular injections. The postoperative wounds were treated with sulfamides. Sulfathiazole, tibatin, elendron, albucid and atebrin were the m3ost commonly used agents in the treatment of abscesses. Sulphamide treatment was supplemented with vitamin C and E injections. Hormones (Progynon B and Testoviron) were often injected. Such treatment was continued for several

---

[171] T. Musioł, *Dachau...*, op. cit., p. 206.
[172] S. Sterkowicz, *Zbrodnicze...*, op. cit., p. 212.

days until purulent foci formed and signs of total intoxication appeared. Sometimes, after a few weeks, the fever subsided and the patient's condition improved. However, the process of poisoning the body continued[173]. The biochemical treatment was based on the use of 12 therapeutic agents in liquid or tablet form, mainly calcium and phosphorus preparations. Subjects were given either liquid or tablets every hour. If the patient tolerated this, the treatment was repeated. However, patients often developed bloody diarrhoea and vomited blood. They also developed duodenal ulcers, nephritis or jaundice. Careful notes were taken of the treatment every day. The wounds were also photographed every other day[174]. The most primitive and ineffective treatment was homeopathy, which was limited to herbal medicine. Various herbal extracts were used, mostly to treat diseases of the digestive tract. Abscesses were also treated with herbs and body wraps. Nevertheless, people died in the same way as in other wards. They did not suffer from thirst because they were constantly given herbal remedies[175]. There were also amputations of both limbs, kidney operations and trepanation of the skull. In order to keep the patient alive as long as possible, tonics were used to increase the energy of the whole organism or individual organs. The more resistant the patient, the better the treatment. They usually died during the experiment or while being transported to another place with other disabled people[176].

Experiments on the liver were also carried out in Dachau. Research began in the autumn of 1942. Patients with liver and gallbladder diseases or gastrointestinal problems were selected. In some cases, healthy people were also included in the experiments. The studies involved 170 people. All were given daily liver punctures. The surgery involved puncturing

---

[173] D. Jarosiński, *Eksperymenty...*, op. cit., p. 27-28.

[174] Ibidem.

[175] T. Musioł, *Dachau...*, op. cit., p. 209.

[176] Ibidem.

the stomach, small intestine, large intestine or liver. Those who survived the procedure complained of extreme pain[177].

As an experimental site for the German Medical Chamber, a tuberculosis ward was set up in the camp. This place had a number of units, each of which had a different procedure for the treatment of tuberculosis. In one of the units, lime, codeine, strengthening drugs, extra food rations, pneumothorax and surgery were used. Another practice was leaving the sick in beds without treatment or food. Other wards treated patients with gymnastics, walking, cold baths, or homeopathy using herbal tablets, extracts and teas. The breathing method was also applied. The tuberculosis ward was closed in 1942. The number of victims is unknown[178].

In 1939, a blood-crystallising unit was set up in Dachau, where prisoners were given Polygal 10. Many of them died. The unit also produced haemostatic drugs in tablet and liquid form for use in military hospitals to stop the bleeding of wounded soldiers. Soviet and Polish war prisoners were selected as blood donors. Their blood was mixed with vitamins, pectin and fruit extracts to make Polygal tablets or Stryptoral[179].

There was also a surgical ward in Dachau. At first it was not an experimental ward, but later it became one. All surgeries were undiagnosed. Prisoners underwent various types of stomach, gall bladder, appendectomy, hernia, kidney, lung and thyroid operations. Experiments were carried out not only on the sick, but also on the healthy. Research was done for medical experience or for curiosity[180].

The number of prisoners at the Dachau camp is estimated at 5485, of whom 2073 died as a result of the experiments. However, these figures are incomplete as there is no reliable data on all the experiments carried out[181].

---

[177] Ibidem, pp. 210-212.

[178] Ibidem.

[179] http://majdanek.com.pl/eksperymenty/dachau.html (accessed 23/11/2023).

[180] Ibidem.

[181] T. Musioł, *Dachau…*, op. cit., p. 210.

Mauthausen Concentration Camp and Gusen Concentration Camp

The Mauthausen camp was located in the north-eastern part of Austria, about 20 kilometres east of Linz. It was established on 8 August 1938, shortly after the Anschluss, the annexation of Austria by the Third Reich. It was originally intended for political prisoners, but as the war progressed and Germany expanded, it became a place to hold various groups of prisoners, including Jews, communists, homosexuals, clergy and prisoners of war. As in other camps, conditions in the camp were extremely harsh and brutal. Prisoners were forced into slave labour for back-breaking jobs such as quarrying and weapons production. One of the harshest parts of the camp was the quarry, where prisoners worked hard to extract stone. Working on starvation rations was almost impossible. There were 56 subcamps, of which Gusen was the largest. An estimated 335,000 people were imprisoned and forced to work. At least 90,000 prisoners died in Mauthausen, Gusen and other subcamps. Half of them died four months before the camp was liberated[182] by American forces on 5 May 1945.

Medical experiments were carried out here on a smaller scale. They claimed fewer victims, estimated at around a thousand. Some of these experiments were initiated by the camp doctors themselves, but most were part of a regular operation run by the Waffen-SS Hygiene Institute in Berlin. Experiments to treat tuberculosis, typhus and pneumonia were carried out in a number of camps at the same time[183].

The first experiments took place in 1940. Not only sick, but also healthy prisoners were operated on. Between 1940 and 1943 almost all the camp doctors became interested in surgery. It was an unhealthy obsession, which they tried to make look like scientific research. Despite their complete lack of scientific

---

[182] https://mauthausen-memorial.org/pl (accessed 01/12/2023).

[183] S. Dobosiewicz, *Mauthausen-Gusen. Obóz zagłady*, Warszawa 1977, p. 353.

knowledge, they carried out apparently innovative operations to discover new aspects of surgery that would be useful in wartime[184]. The most dangerous surgical experiments were carried out by Dr H. Richter, who experimented with the fusion of the large and small intestines. He photographed every stage of the operation and asked the Polish doctors to provide him with professional reports on their work. He operated on stomachs, kidneys, livers and cut out sections of the brain. Within a few weeks he had caused the death of some 300 prisoners[185].

In late 1942 and early 1943, the first major experiments were carried out in the tuberculosis ward of the Gusen camp. Prisoners were massively infected with tuberculosis, and some were killed by intracardiac injections of phenol. A doctor carried out the 'treatment' of the sick with radiologically proven lung lesions. The patients were given a medicine '101', small dark red granules with a bitter taste. It was prescribed and dosed personally by SS doctors. The drug caused nausea, headache, vomiting, diarrhoea, anorexia and muscle aches. Patients were carefully examined before starting treatment and every two weeks during treatment. Tests for Koch's mycobacteria, a lung X-ray, blood and urine tests were carried out, the patients' weight was recorded and they were asked about their general wellbeing. The results were negative. Patients' body temperatures rose, lesions in the lungs widened and coughing developed. People were dying, but the experiments continued. The study lasted a year and a total of 300-400 prisoners were subjected to the 'treatment'. Apart from a few isolated cases, no positive effect of the drug was found[186]. Between 1944 and 1945, the experiments on tuberculosis patients were continued by Dr H. Vetter. On his orders, the tuberculosis ward was closed and most of the patients were killed by lethal injection. A small group was kept alive for further experiments. This group was treated with ruthenium pellets.

---

[184] Z. Wlazłowski, *Przez kamieniołomy i kolczasty drut*, Kraków 1974, p. 40.
[185] J. Osuchowski, *Gusen – przedsionek piekła*, Warszawa 1961, p. 192.
[186] S. Dobosiewicz, *Mauthausen…*, op. cit., p. 356.

No documentation of medical experiments on tuberculosis patients in Gusen has been found. Several hundred prisoners died as a result of the experiments[187].

Spotted fever was researched on a large scale, and initially involved studying pleghmon. Prisoners were injected with pus taken from patients suffered from pleghmon and then treated with a remedy. In 1943, doctors included these patients in research on spotted fever vaccines using antitrypan serum. Systematic experiments with spotted fever were carried out by the last camp doctor, Dr H. Vetter. He was interested in the effects of sulphamides, mainly because of their antibacterial properties. He used them on diseases associated with high fever - typhus, spotted fever, rubella, pneumonia, influenza, tuberculosis and abscesses. He carried out his experiments on the sick and selected healthy prisoners, whom he infected by applying bacteria. He conducted his research on a group of patients who were treated and a group of patients who were not. By comparing patients from both groups, he was able to study the effect of the remedy. Doctors were required to take detailed medical histories of prisoners who had been experimented on and, if a patient died, to carry out a thorough autopsy[188].

Food research was also carried out in Mauthausen/ Gusen to find the most suitable type of food for concentration camp inmates. The broader study was conducted between 1943 and 1944 and involved two options. The first was to replace natural protein. The second was to feed the prisoners food with different levels of protein. In July 1943, 450 healthy prisoners of different nationalities were selected and divided into three groups. For 6 months they ate meals in which natural protein was replaced by cellulose. This was made from wood waste from the production of cellulose at the nearby Lezinger textile factory. The cellulose produced in this way was used to make a sausage called 'Mycel-Eiweisswurst'. The results are unknown.

---

[187] Ibidem.

[188] S. Dobosiewicz, *Mauthausen...*, op. cit., p. 357.

The prisoners probably suffered gastrointestinal problems and died as a result of eating 'the cellulose protein'. In the end, the experiment was unsuccessful[189].

In a second study, carried out from 1 December 1943 to 31 July 1944, 370 prisoners were selected. They were divided into three groups and given different types of food:
- the first group, labelled A, was fed a protein-free, so-called eastern food (150 people),
- the second group, labelled B, was given rations supplemented with beer yeast (110 people),
- the third group, labelled C, was fed 'normal' camp food (110 people).

Throughout the experiment, the prisoners had their blood and urine samples taken and analysed regularly, their weight monitored and ECGs carried out. It resulted in severe stomach ache and extreme weakness. During the study, 56 prisoners from group A, 17 from group B and 43 from group C died. It is impossible to say how many died as a result of the experiment, as some of the prisoners were ill. Another 48 people were sent to the 'treatment centre' at Schloss Hartheim to be killed[190].

Ravensbrück Concentration Camp

Ravensbrück Concentration Camp was the largest women's camp in Germany. It was built before war broke out, in November 1938, north of Berlin. It was a women's camp. In April 1941 a small men's camp was established next to it. The community of prisoners was multinational and represented more than 30 different countries. Most came from Poland (36%), followed by the Soviet Union (21%), the German Reich (18%, including Austria), Hungary (8%), France (6%), Czechoslovakia (3%), the Benelux countries (2%) and Yugoslavia (2%). The number of prisoners is estimated

---

[189] Ibidem.
[190] http://majdanek.com.pl/eksperymenty/mauthausen.html (accessed 03/12/2023).

at about 132,000, of whom about 50,000 died. The camp was liberated by the Red Army on 30 April 1945[191].

Medical experiments were carried out on women and young girls. Two categories of medical research in Ravensbrück[192]:
- research into sulphonamide treatment of gas gangrene, staphylococcus aureus or tetanus (first deliberately induced in women),
- research into the regeneration of bones, muscles and nerves, research into bone transplants.

The first experiments began in June 1942, when healthy patients were deliberately infected with gas gangrene. This was done by making an incision in the skin and introducing bacteria. Initially, prisoners from Sachsenhausen Concentration Camp were used, but due to difficulties in transferring prisoners, it was decided to continue the experiments on female prisoners in Ravensbrück and to extend the research. As a result, the camp began to carry out[193]:
- treatment of typhoid fever with urine enemas of pregnant women,
- additional surgeries to improve the surgical practice of the camp doctors.

In addition, female prisoners from this camp were used in experiments at the Dachau camp, where they used their bodies to warm up prisoners who had been taken out of the freezing water (see above).

Research into gas gangrene focused on the effectiveness of sulphonamides, a group of drugs designed to stop the growth of anaerobic and pus-forming bacteria. Gas gangrene, Staphylococcus aureus and tetanus were the most commonly used bacteria in the studies. The bacteria were injected directly into the lower limb. Another method was to cut the

---

[191] https://encyclopedia.ushmm.org/content/en/article/ravensbrueck (accessed 30/11/2023).

[192] H. Klimek (ed.), *Ponad ludzką miarę. Wspomnienia operowanych z Ravensbrück*, Warszawa 1986, p. 10.

[193] http://majdanek.com.pl/eksperymenty/ravensbruck.html (accessed 24/11/2023).

skin and insert the bacteria into the wound. Muscles were crushed to induce necrosis and help the bacteria grow[194].

The experiments began on 1 August 1942. After consultation with the Waffen-SS Hygiene Institute, it was decided to fill the wounds with sand, wood shavings, glass and metal pieces to simulate the wounds of soldiers fighting at the front. In each group, some women were treated with sulphonamides, while others received no treatment at all. Five women died as a result of the experiments. The study was concluded with a report of no effectiveness of the sulphonamides in the treatment of gas gangrene[195].

Much of the research in Ravensbrück involved experiments in bone regeneration and transplantation. There were three types of bone surgery in the camp, where bones were broken and transplanted, and then the process of fusing and receiving broken limbs was studied. Bones were brutally broken with hammers and chisels. They were then reassembled with or without special connectors, sutured and bandaged. The plaster was removed early after a few days to see how quickly the bones had fused together. The experiments were repeated several times on the same people. One person had five operations[196].

---

[194] Ibidem.

[195] U. Wińska, *Zwyciężyły wartości. Wspomnienia z Ravensbruck*, Gdańsk 1985, p. 256.

[196] http://majdanek.com.pl/eksperymenty/ravensbruck.html (accessed 24/11/2023).

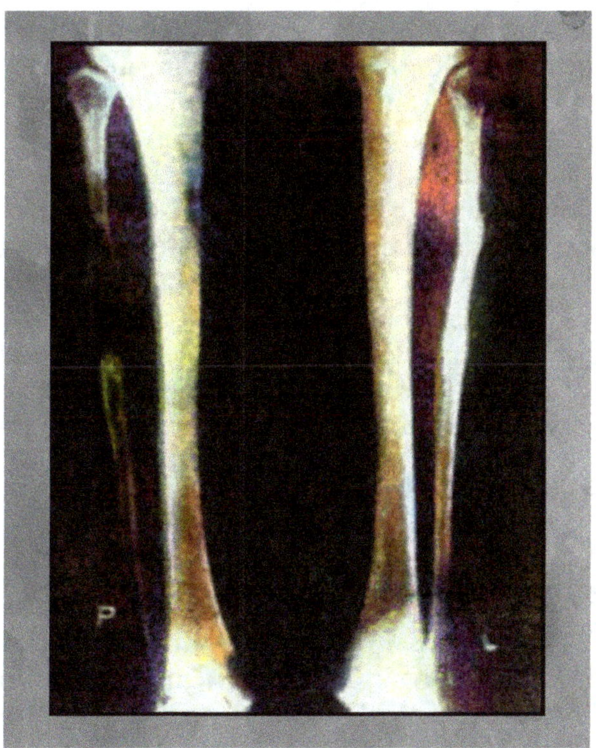

Photo 15. Effects of the experiments. Tibia bone of a female prisoner of Ravensbrück Concentration Camp[197].

Some of the tests aimed to collect bone strips. These experiments consisted of cutting a 2x5 cm rectangle in two places on the tibia, and then, parts of the bones surrounding this rectangle were cut out. In this way, they wanted to investigate the process of bone regeneration. The procedure was based primarily on X-rays. In the camp, attempts were also made to transplant tibia bones from the right leg to the left and back again, to transplant fibula bones in place of tibiae, and to amputate entire limbs (including the hip joint or scapula). The collected limbs and bone strips were wrapped in sheets and then transported to hospitals in Germany, where they were probably implanted into wounded German

---

[197] Photo: public domain.

soldiers. The exact results of the bone surgeries are not known, however, because the experimenters never published them[198].

In this camp, research was also carried out on nerves and muscels to analyze how quickly they could regenerate, which was important for plastic surgery. However, relatively few of these experiments have been performed. The nerves or muscles of the thigh were repeatedly cut out, and each time larger samples were taken, which led to extensive defects in the limbs. 74 Polish women, one Ukrainian, one German and ten mentally ill women of different nationalities were subjected to experiments[199].

Sterilisation procedures were also carried out in the camp. About 800 Jewish women were transferred from Ravensbrück to Auschwitz for experimental purposes. As enemy troops approached, some of the victims were taken back to Ravensbrück. In January 1945, Dr Clauberg arrived at the camp and, together with the camp doctors, continued the experiments, mainly on young Gypsy and Jewish women. The number of victims is unknown, as most died in the gas chambers. The experiments consisted of injecting contrasting fluid into the fallopian tubes (under radiological control) to test their patency. After a few days, the fertility deprivation was continued with the injection of an irritant fluid (including formalin). After 4-8 weeks, a follow-up examination was performed to check the degree of fusion of the fallopian tube lumen. At the end of a year, the women were to have sexual intercourse to test the effectiveness of the method. As the end of the war approached, the study was discontinued[200]. Research on sterilisation was also carried out by Dr. H. Schumman, who had originally worked in Auschwitz. His method involved regular exposing the reproductive organs of men and women to X-rays (3-4 times a week). During this experiment, both the duration of exposure and the intensity of the radiation were varied in order to obtain optimal rates. After the treatment, the victims returned

---

[198] Ibidem.

[199] Ibidem.

[200] H. Klimek (ed.), *Ponad ludzką miarę…*, op. cit., pp. 14-15.

to work. A few weeks later they were examined again, often with surgical castration to collect histopathological material. Approximately 120-140 Gypsies were subjected to radiography[201].

Initially, operations were carried out under aseptic conditions in operating theatres. As the women's resistance grew, the operations were moved to barracks. SS men gagged the women's mouths and held their legs. Hygiene rules were not followed.

In addition to biological experiments, a number of other completely unjustified operations were carried out, such as stomach resections and removal of the thyroid gland.

They were intended to extend the medical practice of the camp doctors. Adrenal glands were removed from epileptics and transplanted into asthmatics with bronchial problems. The central part of the ovaries or the whole ovaries were removed for sterilisation. Studies were also carried out on malaria, and enemas were performed on patients suffering from spotted fever using the urine of pregnant women. The report noted that 30 women participated in the study, but no changes were observed, neither improvement nor deterioration in health[202].

Sachsenhausen Concentration Camp

Another camp where experiments were carried out on a larger scale was Sachsenhausen Concentration Camp, which was established before the war in July 1936 (about 30 kilometres north of the Reich's capital, Berlin). It operated until 22 April 1945. It was a training ground for German concentration camp staff, including those responsible for criminal practices in all the camps. In the almost nine years it ran, some 200,000 people passed through. As in the other camps, the largest groups of prisoners were Poles and Russians[203]. Sachsenhausen held people of 40

[201] Ibidem.

[202] https://mp.pl/auschwitz/journal/english/170062,pseudo-medical-experimens-in-hitlers-concentration-camps (accessed 26/11/2023).

[203] Sachsenhausen held some two hundred thousand prisoners, including 70,000 Poles, half of whom died in the camp.

nationalities. The exact number of victims is unknown, but it is estimated that tens of thousands of prisoners died there from disease, starvation, executions and medical experiments[204].

Initially, the place was a transit camp for German opponents of Nazi ideology, and later for many clergymen who were held there before being sent to other German concentration camps[205].

Human experimentation was also carried out in this camp. Infectious diseases, purulent infections, racial aspects and injuries caused by poison gas were studied. Surgery was performed on prisoners suffering from urological problems without any legitimate medical indication[206].

On 8 September 1939, just a week after the Wehrmacht invaded Poland, retreating Polish troops accidentally used sulphur mustard[207] instead of standard explosives to blow up a bridge in Jasło. This unfortunate incident resulted in 14 German soldiers being poisoned by mustard gas, two of whom died. The incident prompted an immediate response from German chemical weapons experts. The Military Medical Academy and the SS undertook the number of tests to assess the possibility of treating skin wounds caused by mustard gas, conducting at least two series of experiments at Sachsenhausen Concentration Camp on a total of 31 prisoners. The experiment involved deliberately inducing wounds by applying an oily form of iperite directly to the skin of the victims and then treating them with preparations labelled 'H' (after the inventor of the drug, Holzmann), 'F-1000' and 'F-1001'. The prisoners' wounds were also infected with various bacteria, including streptococcus, staphylococcus and pneumococcus. The first experiments ended on 22 December 1939. The post-experiment report proved that the victims suffered from sepsis (general infection). It is noteworthy that none of the remedies

---

[204] https://myslpraska.pl/sachsenhausen-1939-1945-niemiecki-oboz-koncentracyjny-by-nie-zapomniec/ (accessed 28/11/2023).

[205] Ibidem.

[206] Zegarski W. 'Szpital w Sachsenhausen na tle warunków obozowych w latach 1940–1945'. Przegląd Lekarski. 1965; 1: pp. 75-86.

[207] Sulphur mustard - mustard gas.

provided relief from iperitic wounds. It was also found that non-infected wounds had a better ability to heal themselves than infected wounds[208].

The experiments were repeated in 1944. Eight prisoners were treated with mustard gas on both arms. Two prisoners had their wounds opened and infected with a mixture of bacteria after three days. Wounds measured 7 x 18 cm. The infected prisoners developed sepsis with high fever, chills, swollen glands and enlarged spleen. Neither Holzmann's nor Freskan's 'F-1000' and 'F-1001' were effective in treating mustard gas wounds or other infections[209].

On 11 September 1944, an experiment was carried out to see whether placing aconitine in bullet would cause the death of victim, even in the case of harmless shots. Aconitine, one of the most powerful poisons of plant origin, causes paralysis of the respiratory centre or cardiac arrest. In the experiment, five Soviet prisoners of war were shot in the thigh, all of whom died in front of the German crew. From a medical point of view, the experiment brought no new scientific knowledge, as the effects of aconitine poisoning had been known in medicine since the Middle Ages.

Prisoners were also given poisonous potassium cyanide to see how long it would take them to die. This was done between 1944 and 1945. No details available[210].

Hepatitis was the subject of another experiment. Children of Jewish origin aged 8-14 were deliberately infected with hepatitis in order to develop a vaccine. The virus was injected intramuscularly through a tube inserted into the duodenum or gastrointestinal tract. The children were also subjected to painful liver punctures during follow-up examinations. Complete results are not available. They probably all survived

---

[208] F. Schmaltz, Chemical weapons research on soldiers and concentration camp prisoners in Nazi Germany [in:] https://link.springer.com/chapter/10.1007/978-3-319-51664-6_13 (accessed 27/11/2023).

[209] Ibidem.

[210] http://majdanek.com.pl/eksperymenty/sachsenhausen.html (accessed 27/11/2023).

due to the bombing of the camp and the end of the war[211].

Other experiments carried out in the German camp involved research into purulent infections. In 1943, Dr Emil Christian Schmitz induced infections by cutting open a healthy limb and introducing a purulent substance into it. He then experimented with treatments whose effectiveness was not yet known. According to available sources, these experiments were initiated by Dr Schmitz himself and involved about 25 people. The number of people who died is unknown. An eyewitness, Bruno Rőhr, a nurse in the camp infirmary, reported that 18 prisoners died as a result of these gruesome experiments[212].

In turn, the court records of the Sachsenhausen camp staff show that in 1943 the camp doctor, Dr Heinz Baumkőtter, conducted an experiment on three prisoners to test an unknown drug to slow down the heart rate. Substances were administered to the prisoners from ampoules marked 'A', 'B' and 'C'. One of the victims reported that at least one person died. The experiment was probably commissioned by a pharmaceutical company to test the effectiveness of a new drug. The three vials may have contained the same drug in different concentrations. No detailed results are available[213].

Other experiments included attempts to treat tuberculosis by inhalation and to treat kidney stones by dissolving them. Research was also carried out in the camp to identify specific traits that might influence racial differences.

There was also a penal company in the camp that tested the durability of footwear and the effects of stimulants. The prisoners marched along a specially prepared road wearing the new shoes, carrying a 30 kg load and covering at least 30 km a day in 10-12 hours. Some of the prisoners were given stimulants and then forced to continue walking at night to see if their physical capacity increased. There is no data on the number of prisoners in this camp

---

[211] https://mp.pl/auschwitz/journal/english/170062,pseudo-medical-experimens-in-hitlers-concentration-camps (accessed 27/11/2023).

[212] http://majdanek.com.pl/eksperymenty/sachsenhausen.html (accessed 28/11/2023).

[213] Ibidem.

who were subjected to this type of experiment[214].

It is interesting to note that after the end of the Second World War, the Soviets imprisoned Nazi activists, political prisoners and their soldiers here. The Sachsenhausen camp was transformed into NKWD Unit No. 7, where about 60,000 people were imprisoned, of whom 12-13,000 died by 1950[215].

Cruel practices were also carried out in other camps. Sources report that in the camps of Stutthof, Flossenbürg, Majdanek, Munich, Natzweiler-Struthof, Neuengamme and Gross-Rosen various surgical procedures were carried out to improve medical practice. These included operations on the stomach, liver, kidneys and brain. On a smaller scale, infectious, gynaecological and toxicological experiments were also carried out. 'Specialists' deliberately infected healthy prisoners with various diseases: spotted fever, malaria, smallpox, typhoid, viral hepatitis, cholera, diphtheria. Another practice at the Gross-Rosen camp was the use of corrosive liquids on those killed in the gas chambers, and samples taken from their clothing and equipment for testing. All this was done to find the most effective methods of disinfection and insect control under front-line conditions.

According to one source, a total of 27,759 people were victims of medical experiments and 4,364 people died as a result or were killed immediately afterwards[216].
Unfortunately, the data presented may be inaccurate, as research was not always reported. In addition, some facts were not recorded in reports, and documents were destroyed, especially during the liberation of the camps.

---

[214] https://mp.pl/auschwitz/journal/english/170062,pseudo-medical-experimens-in-hitlers-concentration-camps (accessed 28/11/2023).

[215] https://truthaboutcamps.eu/th/zaczelo-sie-w-rzeszy/15472,Zaczelo-sie-w-III-Rzeszy-Obozy-koncentracyjne-na-terenie-Niemiec-1933-1945.html (accessed 27/11/2023).

[216] Weindling P, von Villiez A, Loewenau A, Farron N. *Victims of unethical human experimentation and coerced research under National Socialism.* [in:] https://ncbi.nlm.nih.gov/pmc/articles/PMC4822534/ (accessed 29/11/2023).

Dear reader, this is where I would like to stop. I hope I have made the history of the concentration camps clear in this chapter. I wanted you to know the true facts about Nazi terror. I chose the subject of medical experimentation because it is one that is rarely (if ever) discussed in schools. As I mentioned at the beginning of my publication, I would like to point out that the curriculum is overloaded with historical events from the distant past and history teachers do not have time to discuss the period of the Second World War. If they do manage to do so, it is at the end of secondary school, when students are no longer interested in the past but are already thinking about the future - the upcoming summer holidays or university exams and plans for life after graduation.

In this chapter we learn about the Nazi ideology. The pain, the blood, the fear, the suffering of innocent people, the lack of empathy for others, the crying of children, the degradation of humanity. By understanding the origins of these tragic events, we can turn our attention to the future.

Today, in the modern world, morality, medical ethics and human rights are the foundations on which we base the progress and development of science. Experiments conducted without consent and without respect for human dignity are severely punished and condemned by the community. Learning from the past, humanity is constantly striving to protect human rights and to create mechanisms and institutions to prevent the recurrence of such atrocities. By reflecting on the past and the present, we should build a better world in which respect for life and human dignity is the basis of all human action. We can build a better future, not only in the medical field, but in society as a whole.

Let's move on to the final part of the book, where I present the postwar world.

Conclusion

Europe after the Second World War

The Second World War in Europe ended on 8 May 1945 with the signing of the Act of Unconditional Surrender by Germany. This ended Nazi rule and the Axis Powers - Germany, Italy and Japan - surrendered. The Nazi era was over. On 30 April 1945 (although this remains controversial), Adolf Hitler committed suicide in his Berlin bunker. At 23:01 Central European time, the Act of Surrender came into force.

> In Russia, Victory Day is celebrated on 9 May because it was already 9 May in Moscow.
> The Act of Surrender was signed on 8 May at 11:01 pm, and for the Russians on 9 May at 1:01 am.

The war left Europe completely devastated. The conflict claimed the lives of some 60 million people, both soldiers and civilians. For the first time in history, more civilians than soldiers died as a result of warfare, the most horrific of which was the Holocaust. Many European cities, towns and villages lay in ruins as a result of the intense bombing. Millions of people lost their homes and farms, causing massive population movements. Initially they fled the war (from the Nazis) and then the approaching Red Army. Some were deported because they were unwanted. The effects of the war affected everyone in Europe. After independence, Czechoslovakia expelled almost 3 million Germans from 1945 and Poland 1.3 million. Many children were orphaned. In Yugoslavia, the number reached 300,000. Unwanted pregnancies added to the tragedy, and the extent of the rape of women by soldiers, mainly from the Red Army, is difficult to determine. In Germany alone, some 2 million abortions[217] were carried out each year between 1945 and 1948. In Germany, an estimated 70% of housing was destroyed, and in the Soviet Union 1,700 towns and 70,000 villages were bombed. Factories and workshops lay in ruins, and fields and forests were devastated.

Rebuilding the continent and establishing new political, economic and social arrangements were key challenges. Victory Day in Europe symbolises not only the end of the Second World War, but also the establishment of norms to ensure peace, security and prosperity. At the beginning, the powers decided to create an international institution, more effective than the League of Nations, to prevent conflict and war. The United Nations (UN) was founded in San Francisco in April 1945 by 50 countries. The organisation still exists today[218]. Economic institutions such as the International Monetary Fund and the General Agreement on Tariffs and Trade (now the World Trade Organisation) were also created at this time to prevent potential global crises such as those that contributed to the outbreak of the Second World War.

The Holocaust and other Nazi crimes led countries to want to create a world based on common norms and values. After the war, the International Military Tribunal was established to try crimes against humanity. Today, this function is carried out by the International Criminal Court. Judging Nazi criminals was the main task of the Military Tribunal. The victorious nations established the Universal Declaration of Human Rights in 1948 and the Geneva Conventions in 1949 to protect both soldiers and civilians during wartime.

The Allied effort to rebuild the postwar world on the basis of friendship and respect gave way to a conflict known as the Cold War. The result was the division of the continent into two spheres of influence, separated by the Iron Curtain.

---

[217] https://ciekawostkihistoryczne.pl/2015/06/15/ziemie-odzyskane-gwaltem-w-1945-roku-nie-tylko-sowieci-brali-sila-niemieckie-kobiety-18 (accessed 21/12/2023).

[218] As of 04/06/2024, and there is no indication that the organisation is going to stop operating soon.

COLD WAR - tense political and economic relations between the US and its allies, the USSR and its satellite states, after the Second World War. A conflict that could not be resolved by military action.

IRON CURTAIN – a term used to describe the isolation of areas under the rule of the USSR from the non-communist world. It originates from a speech made by the British Prime Minister Winston Churchill in Fulton, USA (March 1946), in which he called on the United States to oppose Joseph Stalin's policy of expanding Soviet influence and the communist system. This speech is considered the beginning of the Cold War.

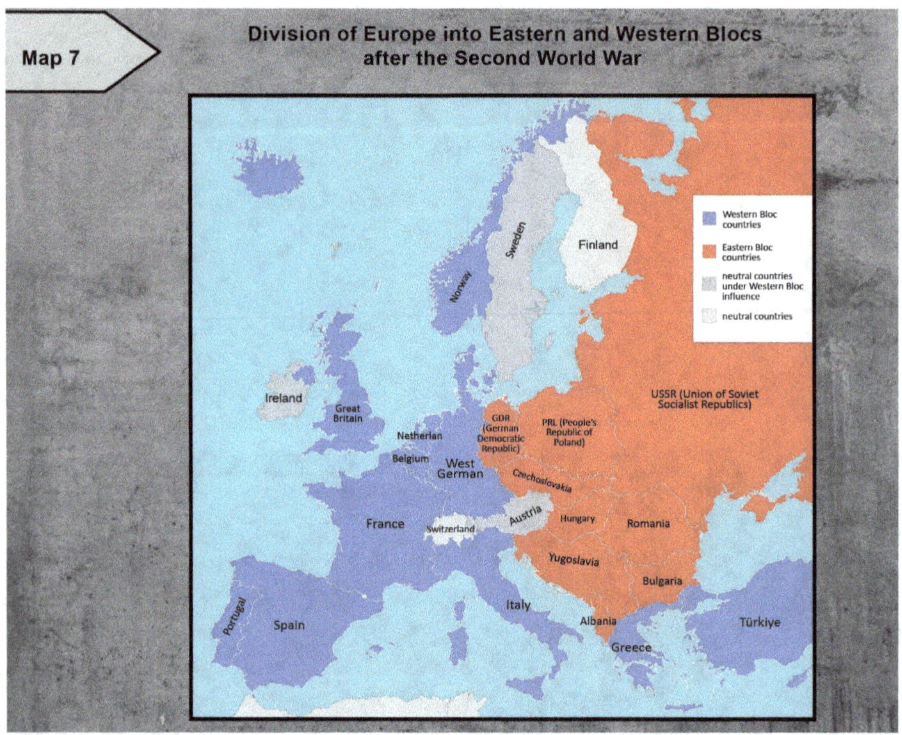

Map 7. Division of Europe into Eastern and Western Blocs after the
Second World War[219]

The Eastern Bloc consisted of countries under a communist regime. The main player on this side of Europe was the Soviet Union. On the map you can see that the satellite countries of the USSR were Poland, Czechoslovakia, Hungary, Romania, Bulgaria, Yugoslavia, Albania and East Germany (soon to be called GDR - more on this below). These countries were deprived of their independence and had to submit unconditionally to the Soviet regime. The Eastern Bloc countries began to cooperate economically through the Council for Mutual Economic Assistance (COMECON). They also formed a military alliance known in history as the Warsaw Pact. Yugoslavia and Albania, on the other hand, marked their independence in the

---

[219]   Map created under the CC BY-SA 3.0 Wikimedia Commons licence, public domain.

context of Soviet influence. Although Yugoslavia was a socialist state, it differed from the other Eastern Bloc countries in that it had a more open policy towards the West. This was because the country was liberated by the partisans under Josip Tito, who played a key role in integrating the different nationalities and ethnic groups in Yugoslavia. On the other hand, in 1961 Albania broke off relations with Moscow and asked for support from the People's Republic of China. As a result, Albania left the Warsaw Pact in 1968 and became independent of Soviet influence.

In contrast, capitalism and democracy were dominant in the countries of the Western Bloc. These countries had a leading ally - the United States. In 1949, the United States and Canada formed a military alliance, the North Atlantic Treaty Organisation (NATO), to compensate for the influence of the Eastern Bloc. Europe received massive financial aid from the US under the Marshall Plan[220]. The money was to be used to rebuild postwar Europe. Only the Western Bloc countries could benefit from the aid. The Soviet Union considered this aid unnecessary and banned its satellite countries from benefiting from the funds. This deprived countries such as Poland, Czechoslovakia and Hungary of funds for their national reconstruction.

The war led to territorial changes. The borders of Central and Eastern European states changed and others were wiped off the European map. The Baltic states (Lithuania, Latvia, Estonia) were incorporated into the Soviet Union. Germany, divided by the Iron Curtain, lived through the Cold War with the front line running through the country from North to South. The Federal Republic of Germany (FRG) was established in the West and the German Democratic Republic (GDR) in the East. German eastern territories and southern East Prussia were lost to Poland (compensation for lost eastern territories) and northern Prussia - Königsberg (Kaliningrad) went to the USSR. Czechoslovakia was forced

---

[220] This amounted to around USD 13 billion.

to cede the eastern province of Carpathian Ruthenia to the USSR but, like Austria, its prewar borders were restored.

It was to be expected that Germany would be blamed for the outbreak of a major world conflict. After the end of hostilities and the signing of the Act of Surrender, Germany was divided by the Allied Powers: the United States, the United Kingdom, France and the Soviet Union. Even before the end of the war in 1943, at the Tehran Conference, the leaders of the three powers, Joseph Stalin, Winston Churchill and Franklin Delano Roosevelt, decided on the fate of the defeated German state. Stalin feared that Germany might regain power. He proposed the complete demilitarisation of the Third Reich. Churchill was more moderate, proposing control and re-education of the Germans and rejecting territorial changes. At the next Yalta Conference (February 1945), the Allies agreed on the final division of Germany into four occupation zones, with an additional zone for France. The Four D's plan (denazification, demilitarisation, democratisation and decartelization) was also adopted to build a new German society. As a result of the Potsdam Conference (July-August 1945), Germany was held fully responsible for the outbreak of the war. The introduction of denazification, democratisation, demilitarisation and decartelization procedures for the country was confirmed.

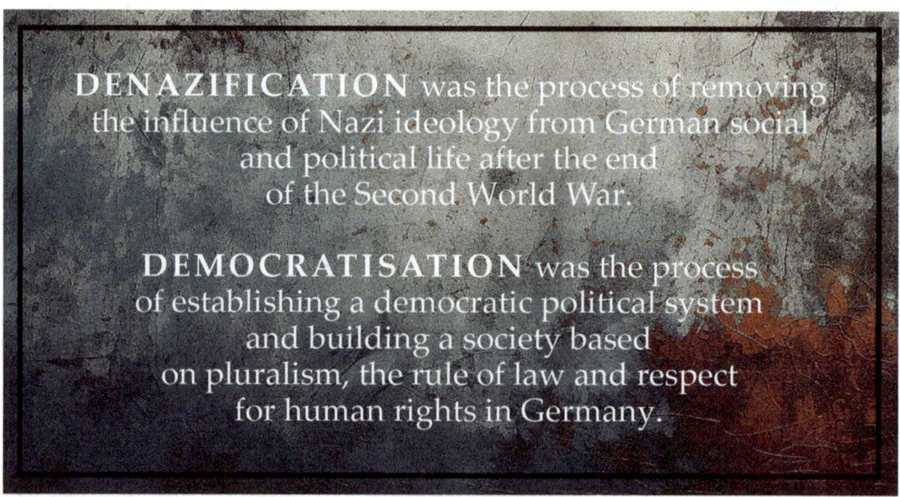

DEMILITARISATION was the process of reducing the military potential of a German country in order to prevent a renewed build-up of its military power. It was a key element of the Allied occupation policy to ensure peace and stability in postwar Europe.

DECARTELISATION was the process of reducing the economic and political power of large German corporations, which were crucial to the German economy and in some ways supported the Nazi regime.

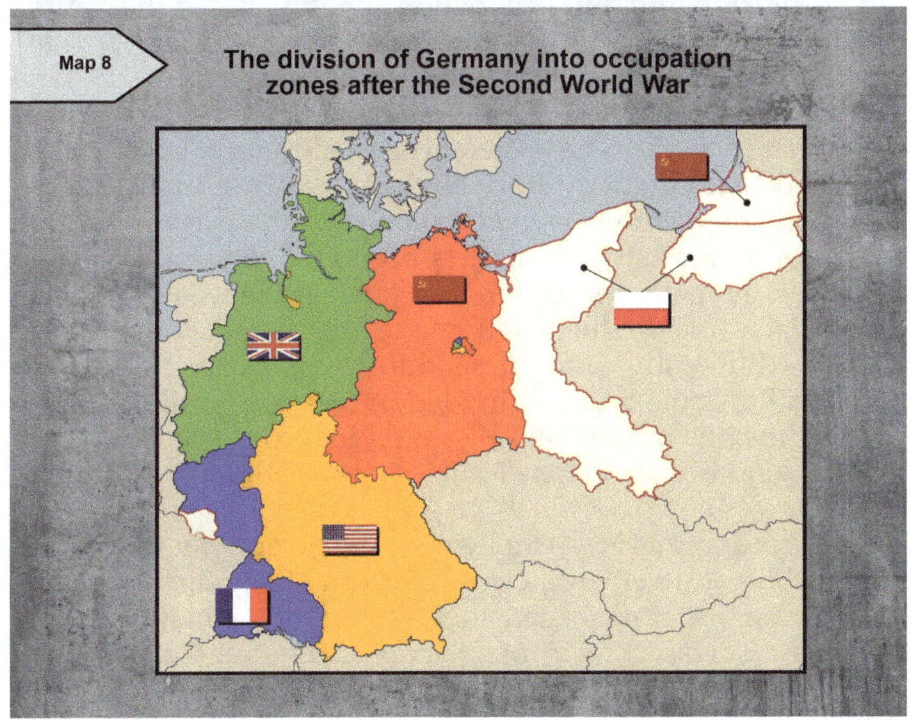

221

The plan of the Four D's was carried out. Map 8 shows the German territory which, after the Second World War, was finally divided into four occupation zones under the control of the major Allied Powers. Detachments were set up in the occupied zones to help restore the German administration. In January 1947, the American and British zones were merged to form known as Bizonia. In April 1949, the French zone joined Bizonia to form Trizonia, which later became the Federal Republic of Germany (FRG). The creation of this country was proclaimed in September 1949. A few weeks later, the Soviets announced the creation of the German Democratic Republic (GDR). Despite ideas of German reunification, political divergence led to a long-term division of the country that lasted until 1990.

The division into four occupation zones included the capital, Berlin.The demarcation line ran through the city and in 1961 the Berlin Wall was built splitting the capital in two. The wall symbolised the boundaries of influence between the Eastern and Western Blocs. The differences in development between West and East Germany were obvious. West Germany's rapid development was due to generous financial aid from western countries, while East Germany's economic development was held back by its disregard for the Marshall Plan. Authoritarian communist rule in the GDR made the two German states develop differently, and these differences were evident for decades. Europe remained divided in this way until the 1990s. At that time, the Eastern and Western Blocs competed with each other in a number of areas - a subject for another publication.

Dear reader, this is where I would like to end my reflections. The turbulent twentieth century brought conflict from the outset. The war that began in 1914 did not initially involve civilians. It was a war of position, aimed at minimising civilian casualties. But it turned out differently than originally envisaged. The First World War claimed up to 9 million lives worldwide. After the war, an epidemic of influenza, known as Spanish flu, killed between 50 and 100 million people.

As a result, Europe was heavily depopulated and had to create a new world order. After the Treaty of Versailles, the League of Nations was established and Poland regained its independence after 123 years of partition. Europe slowly returned to stability. The rulers promised not to let another war break out. Little did anyone know at the time that the First World War was only the beginning of what would happen later in the century. Concentration camps and work camps were set up. The first concentration camp was established in Dachau in Germany in 1933, immediately after the Nazis came to power. This was six years before the war began. Small and large concentration camps, labour camps and later extermination camps were set up. Initially, people who opposed Nazi policies were held. They were imprisoned without trial. Over time, the camps became places of forced labour and regular killing. They existed until they were liberated by the Allied forces. Most of the camps were liberated in 1944 and 1945.

Feeling secure is not just about living in a state with a well-armed military. It is worth looking at the world today and considering what security means to us. For example, we are still exposed to disease and epidemics as we were in the past. In the book, I tried to present Nazi ideology and camp medical 'research' in a simple way. I showed the crossing of the line between scientific experimentation and human morality. I tried to explain the birth of Nazism and the tragic events of that period in a way that everyone could understand. From an insignificant party in Germany to the global dictator. The fascists did a great deal of evil. There is no doubt about the scale of the crimes committed under their rule.

This publication is about what led these people to harm other nations. I have presented their way of thinking and what led them to select people for good or bad. Medical companies that tested drugs on camp prisoners still exist today. Have the cruel experiments and the suffering of innocent people contributed in any way to the development of medicine? Dear reader, you will have to think about this and answer for yourself. But nothing justifies the crimes of 1933-1945.

In conclusion, the current political system and the way the world looks today are, in a sense, a consequence of past events. Would the fascist party never have come to power if there had never been a great economic crisis? Would the Second World War never have happened if Germany's military build-up after the First World War had been under the control of other states? Would there never have been German expansion if Europe had been less lenient with Hitler? We will never know the answer. What if...? We do not know where we would be today if fascist ideology had never emerged.

This is a history lesson that I hope you will find useful and understandable. I hope this book has helped you to understand what was unclear. The history of the First and Second World Wars and their aftermath is our common heritage, worth understanding and remembering. Thank you for joining me on this journey through a turbulent but important period for our civilisation. I believe I have explained the facts and basic concepts clearly and comprehensively. I hope that this book will awaken in you an interest in history as a science in general, whether you are a humanist or a scientist, whatever your profession.

Thank you for joining me on this historic journey.

With kind regards
Dawid Skrobiszewski,
History teacher.

Bibliography and online sources:

- Albert Z. A., Kaźń profesorów lwowskich – lipiec 1941, Wrocław 1989;
- Bandura A., Teoria społecznego uczenia się, Warszawa 2010;
- Behning B., Z badań nad strukturą grup w obozie koncentracyjnym Dachau 1933-1938, Opole 1988;
- Dobosiewicz S., Mauthausen-Gusen. Obóz zagłady, Warszawa 1977;
- Dominiak Ł., Totalitaryzm, [in:] Encyklopedia 'Białych Plam', vol. 17, Radom 2006;
- Dworak T., Totalne państwo narodowe, 'Myśl Narodowa', no. 7 of 14/11/1937;
- Eisler J., Sobańska-Bondaruk M., Historia 1789–1990. A selection of source texts for secondary schools, Warszawa 1995;
- Glad J., Eugenika w dwudziestym pierwszym wieku, 2007;
- Grimm H., Volk ohne Raum, München 1926;
- Hanc J., Homoseksualizm a prawo karne. Analiza synoptyczna, [in:] Czasopismo Prawno-Historyczne, 73(1), Katowice 2021;
- Hitler A., Mein Kampf, München 1943;
- Hoffmann-Curtis K., Memorials for the Dachau Concentration Camp, 'Oxford Art Journal', 1998, vol.21(2);
- Jankowski M., 'Zbrodnicza medycyna w obozach koncentracyjnych III Rzeszy', [in:] 'Papricana'. Humanities journal, 18/10/2012;
- Jarosiński D., Eksperymenty medyczne na ludziach w niemieckich nazistowskich obozach koncentracyjnych, [in:] Studenckie Zeszyty Naukowe, Zeszyt 17, Lublin 2008;
- Kamiński A. J., Hitlerowskie obozy koncentracyjne i hitlerowskie obozy zagłady w polityce imperializmu Niemieckiego, Poznań 1964;
- Klee E., Auschwitz medycyna III Rzeszy i jej ofiary, Kraków 2005;

- Klimek H. (ed.), Ponad ludzką miarę. Wspomnienia operowanych z Ravensbrück, Warszawa 1986;
- Kotłowski T., Problem niemieckich reparacji po I wojnie światowej, Poznań 2014;
- Mikulski J., Medycyna hitlerowska w służbie III Rzeszy, Warszawa 1981;
- Musielak M., Nazizm w interpretacjach polskiej myśli politycznej okresu międzywojennego, Poznań 1997;
- Musielak M., Sterylizacja ludzi ze względów eugenicznych w Stanach Zjednoczonych, Niemczech i Polsce (1899 - 1945), Poznań 2008;
- Musioł T., Dachau 1933 – 1945, Katowice 1968;
- Neumann H. J., Czy Hitler był chory?, Warszawa 2011;
- Nyiszli M., Pracownia doktora Mengele. Wspomnienia lekarza z Oświęcimia, Warszawa 1966;
- Osuchowski J., Gusen – przedsionek piekła, Warszawa 1961;
- Piętka B., Więźniowie z różowym trójkątem w KL Auschwitz [in:] Dzieje najnowsze, rocznik XLVI, Oświęcim 2014;
- Collective work, Autobiografia Rudolfa Hössa, Komendanta obozu oświęcimskiego, Translated by Grzymski W., Warszawa 1989;
- Collective work, Encyklopedia Popularna PWN, Warszawa 2020;
- Rudziewicz A., Eugenika a osiągnięcia współczesnej genetyki, Warszawa 2005;
- Sadowska E., Eugenika a bezpieczeństwo jednostki. Historia myśli, rozwój, przyszłość, Kraków 2018;
- Schmaltz F., Badania nad bronią chemiczną na żołnierzach i więźniach obozów koncentracyjnych w nazistowskich Niemczech [in:] https://link.springer.comchapter/10.1007/978-3-319-51664-6;
- Skrobiszewski D., Pandemie XX i XXI wieku, Bydgoszcz 2012;
- Sterkowicz S., Zbrodnicze eksperymenty medyczne w obozach koncentracyjnych Trzeciej Rzeszy, Warszawa 1981;

- Sugalska I., Eugenika. W poszukiwaniu istoty niemieckiego totalitaryzmu, Poznań 2015;
- Ternon Y., Helman S., Historia medycyny SS czyli mit rasizmu biologicznego, Warszawa 1973;
- Traktat pokoju między mocarstwami Sprzymierzonemi i Skojarzonemi i Niemcami. Wersal 28/06/1919;
- Völklein U., Josef Mengele. Doktor z Auschwitz, Warszawa 2011;
- Weindling P., von Villiez A, Loewenau A, Farron N., Victims of unethical human experimentation and coerced research under National Socialism, Endeavour 2016;
- Widok N., Przeżyć, Wałbrzych 2018;
- Wieliczka-Szarek J., III Rzesza. Narodziny i zmierzch szaleństwa, Kraków 2006;
- Wińska U., Zwyciężyły wartości. Wspomnienia z Ravensbruck, Gdańsk 1985;
- Wlazłowski Z., Przez kamieniołomy i kolczasty drut, Kraków 1974;
- Zechenter A., 'Wyhodować niemiecką bestię', Bulletin 1-2/2023 IPN;
- Zegarski W. 'Szpital w Sachsenhausen na tle warunków obozowych w latach 1940–1945'. Przegląd Lekarski. 1965; 1.
- Documentary 'Lesson Plan' by P. Neel, D. Jeffery 2010;
- http://commons.wikimedia.org/wiki/File:Entwicklung_der_Einwohnerzahlen_in_Deutschland.JPG;
- http://gelsenzentrum.de/kz_buchenwald.htm#KZ;
- http://izrael.badacz.org/galeria/camp.html;
- http://izrael.badacz.org/historia/szoa_obozy.html;
- http://izrael.badacz.org/zydzi_w_polsce/dzieje_rzeczypospolita.html;
- http://majdanek.com.pl/;
- http://old.uwazamrze.pl/artykul/1008252/szkoly-masowego-razenia/3;
- http://ushmm.org/wlc/en/article.php?ModuleId=10005469;

- https://2mecs.de/wp/2008/08/buchenwald-vaernet-experimente-homosexuelle;
- https://auschwitz.org;
- https://ciekawostkihistoryczne.pl/2015/06/15/ziemie-odzyskane-gwaltem-w-1945-roku-nie-tylko-sowieci-brali-sila-niemieckie-kobiety-18;
- https://commons.wikimedia.org/wiki/File:Benito_Mussolini_colored.jpg;
- https://dobrebadania.pl/eksperyment-milgrama-ang-milgram-experiment;
- https://dobrebadania.pl/stanfordzki-eksperyment-wiezienny-ang-stanford-prison-experiment;
- https://facinghistory.org/resource-library;
- https://historia.org.pl/2009/09/07/hanba-monachijska-1938;
- https://ideologia.pl;
- https://lekcja.auschwitz.org/2022_medycyna_pl;
- https://liberte.pl/agnieszka-zakrzewicz-paragraf-175-i-homoseksualizm-wedlug-himmlera;
- https://mapyonline.gwo.pl;
- https://mauthausen-memorial.org/pl;
- https://mp.pl/auschwitz/journal/english/170062,pseudo-medical-experimens-in-hitlers-concentration-camps;
- https://myslpraska.pl/sachsenhausen-1939-1945-niemiecki-oboz-koncentracyjny-by-nie-zapomniec; https://truthaboutcamps.eu/th/zaczelo-sie-w-rzeszy/15472,Zaczelo-sie-w-III-Rzeszy-Obozy-koncentracyjne-na-terenie-Niemiec-1933-1945.html;
- https://natemat.pl/231145,ile-razy-uzyto-haslo-polskie-obozy-smierci-statystyki;
- https://ncbi.nlm.nih.gov/pmc/articles/PMC4822534/;
- https://pafere.org/2021/11/10/artykuly/sprawdz-czy-przypadkiem-nie-jestes-faszysta;
- https://praguemorning.cz/march-15-1939-when-hitler-marched-into-czechoslovakia-RPu7WZG9iE;
- https://racjonalista.pl/kk.php/s,4902;

- https://truthaboutcamps.eu/th/zaczelo-sie-w-rzeszy/15472,Zaczelo-sie-w-III-Rzeszy-Obozy-koncentracyjne-na-terenie-Niemiec-1933-1945.html;
- https://truthaboutcamps.eu/th/zaczelo-sie-w rzeszy/15472,Zaczelo-sie-w-III-Rzeszy-Obozy-koncentracyjne-na-terenie-Niemiec-1933-1945.html;
- https://web.archive.org/web/20091005020549/http://www.time.com/time/magazine/article/0,9171,868574,00.html;
- https://weimar-lese.de/streifzuege/geschichtliches/konzentrationslager-buchenwald; http://judentum-projekt.de/geschichte/nsverfolgung/endloesung/exp.html;
- https://zpe.gov.pl;
https://zwangsarbeit-archiv.de/pl/zwangsarbeit/erfahrungen/lager/index.html.